Words of Praise for Toy Box Leadership

Toy Box Leadership teaches us that sometimes leaders should return to the basic nature of quality leadership by unlocking practical lessons from their childhood toys. This book is a guaranteed a best seller.

> — PAT WILLIAMS
> Senior Vice President, Orlando Magic, author of *Souls of Steel*

Toy Box Leadership made me want to be a young father again so I would have the perfect guide book to do it all over--the right way. Once I read the brief intro in the front of the book I was hooked. I will never look at a Slinky Dog the same way again.

> — KEN MANSFIELD
> Author of *The Beatles, the Bible and Bodega Bay* and *The White Book*

Toy Box Leadership serves as a teaching tool and resource that can be invaluable.

> — DICK VITALE
> ESPN

Discovering things we never knew about childhood toys is one of the fun aspects of *Toy Box Leadership*. Yet, the way they cleverly transmute nostalgia into meaningful lessons of leadership, you'd think the authors were Transformers.

> — SQUIRE RUSHNELL
> Author of *When GOD Winks At You*

Toy Box Leadership does a great job of taking us back to basics and helping us to better understand the importance of the things we learned as we were growing up.

— GERALD E. BODRIE
Retired Executive Director, Logistics Operations,
General Motors Corp.

There are dozens of books about leadership, but Hunter and Waddell offer worthwhile leadership lessons in a particularly memorable way.

— CARTER KEITHLEY
President, Toy Industry Association, Inc.

Toy Box Leadership will leave its fingerprints on the life of each and every reader.

— MATT UPTON
VP of GO "Growth and Opportunities,"
Bell Tasty Foods, INC

Toy Box Leadership presents a realistic approach to unlocking many possibilities for leaders. I recommend it to all who wish to be a more effective leader.

— DR. MELVIN MAXWELL
Founder and President of Park Ministries, Inc.

To build your leadership future, Ron and Michael encourage you to take a look back at your past—at the times and toys of your childhood. It's a great idea—and a great read.

— JOHN D. HULL
President & CEO of ISS and EQUIP

I found myself engaged from the very first words. *Toy Box Leadership* is practical and easy to digest, yet with depth and meaning that produces value for leaders at every level.

— DR. DAN REILAND

Executive Pastor, 12 Stone Church, Lawrenceville, GA.

I never dreamed that toys could be such effective tools for teaching leadership. What an amazing book! The principles in it are powerful.

— DOUG CARTER

Senior VP of EQUIP, author of *Raising More Than Money*

If you think the world doesn't need another leadership book . . . think again, and read this one.

— DR. TIM ELMORE

President of GrowingLeaders.com

Clear, compelling, and chalked full of common sense leadership principles—I couldn't stop reading. *Toy Box Leadership* will give you the essential "toys" to lead in the emerging strengths movement.

— RODNEY COX

Author of *Leading From Your Strengths*

Do yourself a favor and revisit your childhood to learn the timeless laws of leadership. *Toy Box Leadership* is sure to be the most practical, insightful and fun book you read all year!

— LES PARROTT, PhD

Author of *Trading Places*

This book serves up new perspectives and meaningful principles that CEOs and managers will benefit from as they learn to create a more effective workplace that maximizes team spirit and incorporates the best values of the playroom.

— STEVANNE AUERBACH, PHD./DR. TOY
Author of *Smart Play/ Smart Toys* www.drtoy.com

Using simple, well known childhood toys as models, Hunter and Waddell have written a comprehensive book about qualities of leadership, including deep, solid principles and how to apply them.

— R. STEVEN COUCH, MD
Assistant Professor of Pediatrics, Vanderbilt University

Finally, a book that conveys truth with humor. I laughed out loud reading page after page of profound principles reduced to their simplest form. I wish every CEO had this book in his or her "toy box."

— LAURIE BETH JONES
Author of *Jesus CEO, The Path,* and *Jesus, Life Coach*

Toy Box Leadership is one of those great books that come along every once and a while to remind us that we can manage the business of grownup life and still enjoy the wonders of childhood. These concepts are so refreshing—not some set of lofty academic theories but rather practical lessons and principles that can transform you from a passive role-player into a dynamic leader.

— ANDY ANDREWS
New York Times Best-selling author of *The Traveler's Gift*

TOY BOX
LEADERSHIP

LEADERSHIP LESSONS FROM THE TOYS YOU LOVED AS A CHILD

Ron Hunter Jr.
Michael E. Waddell

THOMAS NELSON
Since 1798

NASHVILLE   DALLAS   MEXICO CITY   RIO DE JANEIRO   BEIJING

Published in Nashville, Tennessee, by Thomas Nelson. Thomas Nelson is a registered trademark of Thomas Nelson, Inc.

Thomas Nelson, Inc., titles may be purchased in bulk for educational, business, fund-raising, or sales promotional use. For information, please e-mail SpecialMarkets@ThomasNelson.com.

Library of Congress Cataloging-in-Publication Data

Hunter, Ron, 1967–
    Toy box leadership : leadership lessons from the toys you loved as a child /
Ron Hunter Jr., Michael E. Waddell.
        p. cm.
    Includes bibliographical references.
    ISBN 978-0-7852-2740-3
    1. Leadership. I. Waddell, Michael E., 1968– II. Title.
HD57.7.H8784 2008
658.4'092—dc22   2008002251

Printed in the United States of America

08 09 10 11 12 QW 5 4 3 2 1

Dedication

From Ron

I dedicate this book to my wife, Pamela, who is my best friend and partner in life.

From Michael

This book is dedicated to the memory of my father, R. Eugene Waddell, whose humility was surpassed only by his integrity.

Contents

Introduction

Toys have always been a representation of life. The first toys many of us played with as children were likely little cars, baby dolls, or small workbenches—all models of real life. We copied our parents by doing the things we saw them do, like hammering away at a plastic workbench, driving a Matchbox car down an imaginary freeway, or rocking a baby doll to sleep.

In each case, we utilized actions we would likely use when we grew up and held a real baby, drove a real car, or worked at a real workbench. As children, we played with toys just for fun, but behind the fun we learned how to deal with the reality that was to follow those formative years. The interesting thing about these valuable lessons is that they were all unintentionally learned from toys.

As children, we played with things just for fun, but behind the fun we learned how to deal with the reality that followed those formative years. While people recognize the value of many skills being learned through play, the area of early learning gained through playing with toys that is often the most overlooked is the area of leadership.

As adults, we complicate the principles of leadership with the latest trends or popular theories when in actuality some of the most important lessons we have learned were from the simplest sources and at a very early age. In other words, without consciously knowing it, our childhood toys have already taught us some of the most important leadership lessons we need to succeed.

Toy Box Leadership will take you back to some of the fun and playful benchmarks of your childhood. You will recall the leadership qualities you had as a child that may have been lost along the way. This book is about clearing away the clutter that weighs leaders down and returning to the basic nature of quality leadership by unlocking the lessons from your childhood toys.

LEGO® Bricks

RELATIONSHIPS
Building Begins with Connecting

What would make a corporate lawyer give up his six-figure salary to make thirteen dollars an hour? One word: LEGO®. It all started on Christmas 1978 in Colville, Washington, when five-year-old Nathan Sawaya unwrapped his first set of LEGO® bricks. As the years went by, his collection grew, and his family's living room transformed into a giant "LEGO® city." At age nine, Nathan experienced a life-changing event. His family happened upon a traveling LEGO® tour at the Alameda Square Shopping Center in Denver. Inspired by seeing the grand scale of the White House and the Washington Monument built out of those little bricks he loved, he went back home and built a replica of the Oregon state capitol.

As an adult, Nathan's LEGO® interest was merely a hobby, until 2004, when he entered a contest, sponsored by the LEGOLAND® theme park in San Diego, to find the country's best adult LEGO® builders. He won the contest and left his high-salary job to become a LEGO® master builder, assembling elaborate replicas. Making only one-fifth his lawyer's salary didn't matter to him because he was living his dream.

The history of the LEGO® brick dates back to 1932, in Billund, Denmark, where Ole Kirk Christiansen opened a new carpentry business making stepladders, ironing boards, and little wooden toys. Christiansen called his toys "Lego," a name derived from the Danish words *leg godt* meaning "play well." In 1942, the LEGO® factory burned to the ground. This unfortunate event ended up being a positive one, though, because when Christiansen rebuilt, he chose a plastic injection-molding machine instead of wood to build his toys. In 1949, Christiansen introduced the Automatic Binding Brick to Europe with moderate success. Everything changed in 1961, when the LEGO® bricks were introduced to North America and became an immediate hit. (The LEGO® Group refers to their toys in the plural as LEGO® bricks, not LEGOs®. We will respect their wishes within the chapter.)

It is estimated that more than 235 billion LEGO® parts have been manufactured since the first Automatic Binding Brick was molded in 1949. Today, LEGO® is more than just simple building blocks. LEGO® is toys, theme parks, games, movies, computers, and robots; all sold in more than 115 different countries. Now the fourth-largest toy manufacturer in the world, LEGO® Group employs more than five thousand people and produces more than thirty-three thousand bricks every minute, totaling 16 billion bricks annually. That translates into annual sales exceeding $1.1 billion. *Fortune* magazine recognized this success in 2000, when it named LEGO® the "Toy of the Century."

The popularity of LEGO® bricks results from their versatility. You remember that feeling you had as a child imagining the endless possibilities of what you could build with that pile of LEGO® bricks? Would you venture a guess as to how many ways you can arrange six eight-studded LEGO® bricks? In an astounding 915,103,765 different positions. Now, how many days would that occupy your child?

If you can dream it, the LEGO® Group believes that you can build it. Think about the world records involving LEGO® construction: a 92.5-foot tower using 500,000 bricks; a 4,626-foot-long structure utilizing more than three million components; or a life-size car built out of 650,000 bricks and weighing more than a ton. Each record began by merely connecting two little bricks.

○   ○   ○

LEGO® bricks provide the essence of this leadership lesson on *Relationships: Building begins with connecting.* In business, if you do not connect—with your customer, with your co-workers, with your vendors—you are out of business. Some tremendous products have failed to connect, allowing inferior products to surpass them in sales.

Relationships are the building blocks of any organization. Relationships precede market position, sales goals, research and development, or success in the boardroom. Real influential power relates by connecting. Look at the heart of any successful organization and you will find strong relationships that began because someone cared enough to connect. Relationships or connections will exist at every level in varying degrees and in multiple directions. Connections exist with equal importance inside and outside the organization.

Think of all the connecting that occurs in a single day at your office: people to people, business to business, employees to vision, workgroups to ideas, or management to principles. We connect through e-mail, phone calls, intercoms, heads ducking into doorways, written correspondence, and meetings. And these personal connections represent just a modest percentage of the total connections our organizations actually perform. Think for a minute about how your corporate identity, public relations, and overall image impact others through various means of connections. Each one of these connections is a vital building block for your company's dream.

LEGO® bricks teach us that each individual is interdependent on the next connection for success. The properly placed brick within a structure provides strength and substance and adds to the overall structure. Placing each person so he or she connects properly results in the healthy utilization of human resources. Properly connecting a person within an organization is just as critical to the organization as properly placing a LEGO® brick within a structure. As you remember, one brick stuck in the wrong place can ruin a perfectly good castle.

> Leaders understand the complexity of relationships, and they work to positively develop them.

Leaders understand the complexity of relationships, and they work to positively develop them. As the architect of strong relationships in your organization, you must recognize these three LEGO® leadership categories: Connectional Value, Connectional Ability, and Connectional Failures.

#1: LEGO® Leaders Recognize Connectional Value

Ken Blanchard knows about the value of connecting. He says, "In the past a leader was a boss. Today's leaders must be partners with their people—they no longer can lead solely based on positional power."[1] In other words, your relationships are more important than your position.

Connection is important in every area and at every stage of life. Whether in your neighborhood or at work, you will benefit from building any positive relationship. Whether you are the top dog or the new kid on the block, it is valuable to start making those connections now. Every leader you know has reached that point by making the right connections.

Partnering with your people means treating them with

respect and value. Recognizing their value often begins with understanding their daily job and what they have to deal with to perform it properly. Try working alongside them, if possible, for a while. If their job is technical and not possible for you to do, then observe them while listening to their thoughts on improving their work area or policies affecting them. Get a sense of what they do, what they endure, and what motivates them. If you can energize them, then you have connected. Ivory towers, strong autocratic styles, and smugness among leadership inhibit connection on many levels.

A legal secretary was eating in the cafeteria with other secretaries, a couple of associates, and a partner. This partner understood and possessed the ability to connect. Another partner, passing by and seeing his colleague eating with everyone else, paused in the doorway and chided, "You're slumming it today, huh?" This personality type fails to connect, kills morale, and fosters resentment. He tears down more than he ever builds. He's that LEGO® brick that causes your castle to crumble. Good leaders appreciate the power of professional relationships once they realize the growth possibilities stemming from that connection.

Connecting Builds a Strong Foundation

Nathan Sawaya's largest LEGO® project to date is a replica of a Chris Craft Speedster. It took him more than 180 hours, and he used almost 250,000 bricks. It is more than ten feet in length, and it holds the world record for the largest LEGO® boat. When commenting on his method, he said that building with LEGO® bricks takes a "bottom-up approach."

The same is true with relationships. When you make a connection, it lays a foundation upon which you can build. The more connections you make, the stronger your foundation becomes and the higher you can build. Strong connections prompt people to come to the rescue of fellow team members rather than throwing them under the bus. The bus's bumper has enough dents in it—get people working more closely together and you will see greater accomplishments from cultivating a stronger foundation for your team.

Connecting Unleashes the Power of Synergy

Synergy is a word that is often misused. Synergy is combining the efforts of two or more entities resulting in a greater sum than individual efforts could have achieved. Former prime minister of Israel Golda Meir understood the power of synergy, stating that she "never did anything alone. Whatever was accomplished in this country was accomplished collectively."

Synergy was typified in January 2007 as Steve Jobs presented the iPhone, which was a result of the cooperative efforts of Cingular/AT&T, Yahoo, and Google, to name a few. Verizon passed on making this connection, so Steve Jobs moved on to connect with another powerhouse, AT&T, and ultimately created one incredible gadget that set a new standard in communication.

Connecting Utilizes the Strength of Unity

Board ethics tell us that when a board passes a vote, and a minority votes against it, the minority should vigorously support the action as if they voted for it themselves. Unity is accomplished when one sets aside self and places the greater good ahead of personal agendas. LEGO® bricks are at their best when you step back and see the entire structure rather than the individual bricks. Cultivate the spirit of unity within your organization by helping people understand the stark difference between unity and uniformity. In any environment, connection comes from unity, not uniformity.

> In any environment, connection comes from unity, not uniformity.

The 1992 movie *The Power of One* is about a young English boy named P. K. living in South Africa during the 1940s. As he grows up, P. K. becomes passionate about teaching the natives English. After losing his parents and his closest friend, he is disillusioned until he sees the great effects of his English language schools among the people. The closing scene renders this inspirational statement: "Changes can come from the power of many, but only when many come together to form that which is invincible . . . the power of one."

#2: LEGO® Leaders Recognize Connectional Ability

LEGO® bricks don't join with others simply by chance. Likewise, the best connections don't happen by accident. Pouring out a box of LEGO bricks will not produce a castle; you will just have a pile of bricks. Similarly, relationships at their best are designed, intentional, connected, and built. While many leaders appreciate the relationships in their organization, they fail to connect the appropriate blocks in the right direction.

LEGO® bricks are not like Velcro, latching randomly, even where they are not meant to connect. LEGO designs are intentional in their con-nections, allowing someone who can see the big picture to pull all the parts together. Bringing it together requires the ability to connect the team and to connect *with* the team. What makes these connections possible? The answers can be found in the three distinct reasons LEGO bricks connect so well.

> Bringing it together requires the ability to connect the team and to connect *with* the team.

LEGO® Bricks Are Reliable

It is not coincidental that LEGO® bricks are among the most reliable toys in the world. Technicians perform a variety of tests on LEGO® elements, and they find that only about eighteen out of every million, or 0.000018 percent, fail to pass their quality assurance tests. You know LEGO® bricks can be trusted before you start to build. Likewise, every good relationship is fundamentally based on trust. This is true in marriages, parenting, friendships, serving in a military unit, and working with colleagues. Work-place trust begins with the administration and ultimately the CEO. Policy affects trust. Mid-level management affects trust. If mid-level management does not implement company policy or direction as if they fully believe it, then their team will lose trust in the leader and the direction the organization is heading. When the manager or leader is away, do employees respond the same as if she were still there? If not, it reflects on the lack of trust in their leadership, and the lack of personal responsibility the employees feel for the success of their team, and by extension, their trust of company-wide policies.

Reliability means you trust your workers enough not to look over their shoulders. This lack of trust by management often results in micromanagement, which will further erode the morale of the organization. Micromanagement as a leadership style devalues the overall team and is not far removed from a dictatorship. It implies to the team that they cannot be trusted to do their job without the ever-watchful eye of management.

Likewise, workers must be able to trust you as their leader. You must earn that trust and can just as easily forfeit it. You earn it by getting in the midst of difficult problems and not passing the buck. Your reliability translates into your followers becoming more reliable. No matter your political party affiliation, you had to admire Mayor Rudy Giuliani on September 11. He did not delegate others to assess damages or wait for New Yorkers to take care of themselves. He put on a dust mask and immediately hit the streets, with the people of his office following him. New Yorkers were inspired by his example, earning him trust that horrid day and in the weeks that followed. Those days of connecting may very well have defined his leadership style.

LEGO® Bricks Are Compatible

LEGO® bricks fit together so well because of two basic components: studs on the top and tubes on the inside. When two bricks are pressed together, the tubes grab the studs and hold with a friction-based connection. The interfacing or connecting of these studs and tubes is the secret to the brick's compatibility. LEGO® makes around three thousand different types of elements, and yet they all fit together. You can buy LEGO® bricks from anywhere in the world, and they will fit seamlessly. Even a brand-new brick will fit perfectly with one that was made in 1958. If only computer compatibility were always this simple.

Getting people who work in various departments to fit together is very challenging. Try to make it easy for employees to connect with one another. Ron witnessed the power of connecting people from various jobs during a series of moral-boosting events at his company, Randall House.

> One morning I walked into a break room to find it unusually crowded. The crowd was a result of an employee-initiated pool tournament. The tournament took place over the course of a week, played only on breaks. I found that even people who did not play stopped by to watch. Fifteen minutes around a pool table did more for connection than eight hours in an office.
>
> One manager took the design team to Barnes & Noble for cover-design expeditions while they were working on upcoming trade book concepts. This removed them from their daily routine, built camaraderie, and allowed them to bond as a team.
>
> On a few unique occasions we have shut down operations for something very special, such as reward trips, family outings, and even a volleyball tournament. These excursions cause an uncommon bonding that most organizations say they cannot afford to do. I believe that you can't afford *not* to do this.

LEGO® Bricks Are Reusable

For years, LEGO® has used the advertising slogan "LEGO® is a new toy every day." You can build one structure with your blocks, disassemble it, and reuse the blocks to build something else. Big business often treats people as disposable, when we should look at how to repurpose our people to better fit the future needs of the company and the employee. LEGO® bricks show the value of repurposing or moving people to a different area of the company, because they are one of the few toys you can use to build the arm of a T-Rex one day and a pirate ship the next. Wise leaders understand that in today's climate people must anticipate having to learn to perform new tasks, develop new skills, and alter their job description. As technology grows, the roles of the same people will continue to expand.

Never get comfortable with where you are. Anticipate the inevitability of having to modify or change how you do business to meet your customers' needs. Probably the single greatest book on anticipating change and approaching it with the right attitude is Spencer Johnson's *Who Moved My Cheese?* The four main characters in his book each represent a common attitude people have when they are confronted with change. One of the characters had "realized that the change probably would not have taken him by surprise if he had been watching what was happening all along."[2]

The movie-rental chain Blockbuster is in the middle of a change right now that will determine its long-term viability. Upstart company Netflix has eaten away a significant portion of its market share by offering customers the convenience of having their rented movies delivered right to their homes and computers. Blockbuster could have whined and complained that it was the one who brought you rental movies as you know them. Instead, it chose to alter its method of service by offering the same convenient mail delivery, with a side bonus of the convenience of being able to return the movie to the Blockbuster store and swap it instantly without waiting for the post office to bring another one. They decided to rebuild a portion of their business structure just as you use the same LEGO® bricks in a different manner. This industry should continue to anticipate change. That's the joy of not super-gluing your LEGO® structure together.

#3: LEGO® Leaders Recognize Connectional Failures

We all experience the annoying dysfunction of dropped calls when using a cell phone. Perhaps the only thing worse is a phone message like "We're sorry, all circuits are busy," or everyone's least favorite, "If you'd like to make a call, please hang up and try your call again." When you fail to connect, communication fails, tasks go undone, and frustration hits pinnacle heights. Connection failures are relationship failures that cause setbacks. Here are four connection failures that you should plan to avoid.

Misplaced Bricks

Sometimes people aspire to certain positions or organizations only to realize that it is not their best career fit. A few years ago, a key manager for Randall House tendered his resignation to go to a larger publisher. He was eminently qualified and flourished in this new role with them. He easily could have stayed there his whole career as a rising executive, but he felt like a misplaced brick. Since he never really connected, he returned to us and was welcomed back and remains a valuable director in the future of our organization.

If you misplace bricks by promoting someone to a position that's not a good fit for him, at least one of you will be unhappy with his performance. That person and the organization lose because he is in the wrong spot. Never sacrifice an individual by misplacing him. People should be moved based upon qualifications and capabilities and for no other reason. Misplacement weakens the entire organizational structure.

Forced Bricks

President Dwight D. Eisenhower said, "You do not lead by hitting people over the head—that's assault, not leadership." Just about every leader occasionally makes the mistake of forcing a relationship that just isn't right. When you force a brick, wrong personalities find the wrong positions. Southwest Airlines figured this out years ago. That is why they have the best "out front" people serving customers and the best technical people teaching employees, resulting in everyone naturally fitting where they belong. Coach people on the value and importance of the job they do, even if it's not a glamorous one. On the other hand, creating an unnecessary position for someone just to keep them onboard is not in anyone's best interest either. If the position is not valuable to the company, remove it, but never demean the individual or their position in the process.

You may have heard the funny story about a four-star general who was flying over the Atlantic when his plane stopped for refueling in Iceland. The general was in a hurry, and when the process was taking longer than anticipated, he went to chew out the personnel involved in delaying him. He found a private who had finished fueling the plane and was now draining the toilets through a large hose. In a loud, threatening tone, the general began to criticize his job performance. The private interrupted and said, "Excuse me, sir, I'm a private, I'm stuck in Iceland in the winter, and I'm pumping sewage from an airplane. What can you possibly do to me that's any worse?"

Sometimes we feel like that private, and sometimes leaders act like that general. Neither is healthy for the organization. Do not force anyone to fill a role against their wishes. If they do not embrace the changed role, the organization may not be able to retain them, but forcing a fit is misery for all parties involved.

Isolated Bricks

If you have children, go look under your couch right now and you will probably find a lonely LEGO® brick. When bricks get lost, they are of no use to anyone. A single LEGO® brick holds less value because it cannot fulfill its purpose. Connect isolated bricks and watch the effective building process start. Don't leave people out. A leader never abandons a follower. Just as bricks are only meaningful when they are part of a project, so people only feel worth when they are connected. Connect them within their strengths and communicate often with them.

Unorganized Bricks

Start with a plan to connect in mind. Take time to mentally separate and categorize your team just as you would physically separate and organize your bricks. Consider using the principles found in the little green army men chapter to assist you (chapter 8). Unorganized bricks slow progress, hamper efficiency, and impede results. No matter what you are building, you have to do it one brick at a time. Be intentional about which person you place where. Organizing your people with a strengths assessment will expedite the building of your organization. The methodology of building without these tools is known as trial and error.

The misplacement of bricks or isolated bricks usually results from the lack of organizing. Forcing bricks occurs when emotions, either yours or theirs, get in the way. Should any of these connection failures take place, you run the risk of not utilizing your team properly, wasting time, expending energy needed in other places, or, worse yet, building a deformed structure. Make the right connections for the right reasons.

○　　○　　○

In January 2007, Nick Saban held his first press conference as the new head football coach at the University of Alabama. One of the first questions he was asked concerned the type of offense that he planned to run. The coach said,

> It's very important that you use the players that you have."
> Saban proceeded to tell the story of his days as a high school quarterback in West Virginia. He said, "We were playing at Masontown Valley. Whoever wins the game is getting in the playoffs. We get behind 18–nothing. . . . Come out after halftime . . . and it's 18–12, 1 minute 27 to go in the game. We get the ball back. . . . We get down to 4th and 12 at the 25 yard line. One timeout left. Take it. Everybody in the town where I grew up is at the game. . . . I'm saying, 'Thank goodness Coach Keener is going to call this play, then I won't get blamed for calling the wrong play.' He says, 'I tell you what. You have a three-time all-state split end, the left half-back, fastest guy in the state. I don't care what play you call, just make sure one of those two guys gets the ball.' I call '26 crossfire pass.' Threw it to the left halfback . . . 25 yard touchdown, we won the game 19–18. After the game he told me this, 'It really doesn't make any difference what play you call sometimes; it's what players you have doing it.'"[3]

Leaders often get so caught up in the programs that they forget about the people—the building blocks of any program. While there is tremendous value in plans, the strength of any organization is in its relationships. Remember, building begins with the clicking sound of connections.

One final word about Nathan Sawaya, the lawyer-turned-professional LEGO® artist. Today he is one of the top LEGO® sculptors in the world; his art values range from one hundred dollars to tens of thousands of dollars. LEGO® bricks changed Nathan Sawaya's life. Believe it or not, the lesson they teach could change yours too.

* The term LEGO Leader was coined by the writers without collaboration or cooperation with The LEGO Group. The LEGO Group does not sponsor, authorize or endorse the term LEGO Leader.

2 Slinky® Dog

What walks down stairs, alone or in pairs,
And makes a slinkity sound?
A spring, a spring, a marvelous thing,
Everyone knows it's Slinky® . . .
It's Slinky®, it's Slinky®, for fun it's a wonderful toy
It's Slinky®, it's Slinky®, it's fun for a girl and a boy.

—Advertising Jingle

This cute little song was the first toy commercial to be released as a pop music single. The success of that 1963 record was credited to the immense popularity of the toy as much as it was to the tune. By the way, it will also be stuck in your head all day. In addition to the record, the Slinky® has been involved in a number of firsts. It was the first toy to be used on board the space shuttle for zero-G experiments, the first toy to be given its very own U.S. postage stamp, and the first toy to have its inventor join a cult and move to Bolivia.

The Slinky® has been entertaining people for over sixty years, and even now it continues to grow in popularity. It is hard to imagine with its storied history that the Slinky® came into being by accident. In 1945, Richard James was working as an engineer for the U.S. Navy. He was developing a method to measure horsepower aboard battleships when a tension spring rolled off his desk, hit the floor, and just kept moving. Immediately James saw the potential for this interesting spring to become a very unique toy. It was his wife, Betty, who recommended the perfect name, Slinky®, which is a Swedish word meaning *traespiral,* or sinuous. Betty was also the one who came up with the idea for perhaps the greatest Slinky® toy of all—the Slinky® Dog. The Slinky® Dog got its greatest boost from the 1995 animated movie *Toy Story.*

○   ○   ○

Everybody knows how the Slinky® Dog works, but few of us know why. The law of physics that makes the Slinky® "walk down stairs" and "make a slinkity sound" is known as Hooke's Law. Robert Hooke (1635–1703) observed that when an elastic body is placed under stress, its shape changes in proportion to the applied stress. In other words, when the string attached to the Slinky® Dog's nose is stretched, the dog changes shape—it becomes longer and sleeker—and then as the back end follows the pull, it returns to the original shape, only farther down the road.

If you have ever had a rubber-band war, you understand this principle. Having your sibling in your sights, you instinctively work through a mechanical process of shooting several rubber bands in a matter of seconds. You place the rubber band across the front of your index finger and with the opposite hand stretch it backward—letting it fly toward its target. The same is true with the Slinky® Dog, right down to pulling it where you want it to go. In the *Toy Story* movie, this principle catapulted Slinky® Dog into the moving truck, knocking over his other toy friends.

The Slinky® Dog can open your eyes to the importance of a leader's vision for personal and corporate growth, as it shows you how to attract followers. This toy allows you to observe the responsive process that an organization must go through to achieve growth. The lesson is to pull and then be patient.

More than any other leadership trait, vision pulls an organization forward by giving it direction. A leader at any level who possesses the ability to pull will find followers.

> More than any other leadership trait, vision pulls an organization forward by giving it direction.

You have seen people influence others without necessarily holding a title. Balancing the pull with patience is the tricky part. Leaders find it easy to move, because they're at the front end of the Slinky® Dog; however, it is the back of the organization that is the most difficult to budge. As a leader you will always find the early adopters moving with you, but how you respond to those who lag behind makes a difference in the cohesion of your entire team.

An old leadership proverb teaches, "If you think you are leading and you look behind you and no one is following, you are just going for a walk." One place you do not want to be is so far ahead of your followers that you find yourself alone. People will maintain the pace of keeping up as long as there is a close connection with the leader and his or her excitement about the move. When you get too far ahead, those who follow get lost, and that formerly excited follower turns into a frustrated follower—if he follows at all.

This toy was the inspiration for the whole book. Follow along as Michael retells the story:

Ron and I were on the phone discussing his vision for our company, Randall House. The company was in the middle of some serious growing pains as it moved in a new direction. We were making progress, but the bold move had put our production schedule behind, thus raising the cost of goods and hurting our bottom line. Financially, we were about nine months behind where we had estimated we would be, even though we had sold a lot of product. Ron was looking for a simple illustration to use in his annual report to the board of directors and stakeholders to explain this seemingly slow pace.

I had just watched the *Toy Story 2* movie the night before, and I remembered the scene where the Slinky® Dog is being pulled behind the moving truck. When he is finally stretched to capacity, he shouts, "Buzz, Buzz! My back end's going to Baton Rouge!" And then he finally springs forward back into the truck. I said, "Ron, what you are going through is like the Slinky® Dog. You have pulled the organization forward, and now you have to wait for the back end before you move forward again. Simply tell them you have stretched with vision and to be patient as the profits catch up to the vision."

This principle has been proven to be true at Randall House and in each of our respective careers.

The pulling and catching-up balance is delicate, and you won't always get it right. As you pull with vision, energy is stored up, and when the energy level is just right, it is released, sometimes explosively, resulting in the movement of people. They can literally spring into action, responding to the pull of your vision. How often have you heard people explain

How often have you heard people explain why something can't work rather than trying to figure out how it can? Visionary leaders talk about possibilities rather than improbabilities.

why something can't work rather than trying to figure out how it can? Visionary leaders talk about possibilities rather than improbabilities.

The Process of Pulling

NASA's Apollo rockets used most of their fuel exiting the earth's gravity and then counted on the gravity of the moon to pull the ship toward it. Not only will vision launch your organization to new levels, but it will serve as the gravitational pull keeping everyone on course. "A compelling vision must be so clear and so powerful that its very magnetism and gravitational force will literally pull you towards it."[1]

A leader must see where the organization needs to go and then "pull" it in that direction. It is obvious why we chose the word *pull* rather than *push*. Try pushing the Slinky® Dog from behind and see how difficult he is to steer. A visionary pull is a must, and there are four parts to achieving this.

1. Pull Through Communication

Effectively communicating vision is more than hanging a mission statement in the lobby. Theodore Hesburgh emphasized, "The very essence of leadership is that you have to have a vision. It's got to be a vision you articulate clearly and forcefully on every occasion. You can't blow an uncertain trumpet."[2]

People must know where you are going in order to follow you. Would the Soviet Union have torn down the Berlin Wall had President Reagan not demanded it to the world? Would we have put a man on the moon if President Kennedy had not communicated this vision to Americans? Most major accomplishments are preceded by a communicated vision. Until a communicator with a passionate vision challenges us to do something great together, many times we struggle to find a meaningful purpose.

Communicating the vision is achieved when it is driven deep into the organization, but we do not repeat our vision often enough for our people to take ownership. Patrick Lencioni warns that executives "make the dangerous assumption that once a message has been heard, it is both understood and embraced by employees . . . after communicating it once or twice."[3] How many times do you think those around you must hear a message before they can transfer it to their coworkers? The accepted average is around seven. Now, how many times have they heard you say it?

Chrysler Corporation would not be here today if one of the greatest communicators of vision, Lee Iacocca, then chairman of the board, had not passionately communicated the potential growth of this struggling automaker. While others were predicting its demise, he clearly articulated his vision within his organization and to the public like this: "Quality, hard work, and commitment—the stuff America is made of. Our goal is to be the best. What else is there? If you can find a better car, buy it." This challenging yet simple statement communicated a high standard and pulled his employees to perform with excellence. It was a historic turnaround. Today Chrysler produces some of the most sought-after auto designs. Vision communicates "what could be," and then "what could be" becomes what people do.

Do those around you know your vision? As an aid to four U.S. presidents, David Gergen experienced the power of vision invested in people. He observed, "A leader's role is to raise people's aspirations for what they can become and to release their energies so they will try to get there."[4] How do you raise people's aspirations? You tell them what they are capable of and then recognize their progress along the way.

2. Pull with Courage

Vision can be scary. It is difficult to be the only one in the room who sees where the organization needs to go. Sometimes you may not have the courage to share the "what ifs" of a vision. What if our organization did X? Where would X take us? Since X (your vision) is risky, it requires real courage to pull the group into new territory. It may be tempting to keep the vision to yourself in fear of how your team will react, but that can result in your feeling discouraged because no one can help you get there. And that discouragement can cause you to abandon solid goals.

In the 1980s, it was bold of Apple to break from the mainstream and introduce the Mac computer platform that operated with one click of the mouse rather than several keystrokes. Mac had a windows-type operating system over a decade before Windows 95 was released. Bold steps like this took Apple stock on quite a ride over the years, and whether you are a Mac or PC user, you must admire their adventurous courage. Those who created the Mac and other revolutionary Apple products took the advice of Ralph Waldo Emerson, who said, "Do not follow where the path may lead. Go instead where there is no path and leave a trail."

Blazing new paths usually leads you to what others refer to as "risky territory." Those who do not understand where you are going may label your vision as risky. When this happens, it is a reminder for us to communicate even more consistently. No one wants to follow a leader when they have no idea where they are being asked to go. We reduce the perceived risk or turn it into a wise risk when we share the vision and allow others to add to the vision.

When you are looking for the location of a store in the mall, you go to the directory for a map of all the stores. And when you finally find the store you are looking for, there is one vital piece of information you still need—that little yellow and black diamond-shaped sign saying, "You are here." Leaders show people where they need to go, but they also have the courage to tell them where they are *right now*. Clear communication points out the origin and the destination with a courageous plan to connect those dots.

3. Pull by Example

Unless the head of the Slinky® Dog moves in a certain direction, the rest of it will never go there. Leaders do not send their people out where they are not willing to go. You may remember the classic commercial with three brothers sitting around the breakfast table. The two older brothers are arguing over eating a bowl of this new healthy cereal. Neither wants to take the first bite. As they look across the table at their younger brother, they utter the now famous phrase, "Let's get Mikey. He won't like it, he hates everything."

Many leaders find doing certain tasks in their organization beneath them. Leaders must by example pull others toward accomplishments, even when others are afraid of taking the first bite. Never send them down a road you would not travel yourself—that is the low road of a poor leader. When faced with the choice of being an example or not, our good friend Tim Owen always says, "You will never regret taking the high road by doing what is right." High-road traveling is a model for others, not to mention it allows you a good night's sleep.

Charles Reade, the nineteenth-century English novelist, wrote, "Example is contagious behavior." When you step up and reach beyond your normal duties, it sets a tone for others to see. Ron experienced one leader within the organization doing just this:

One of our products was featured on a live radio broadcast, and we received so many calls it shut down our switchboard for a few moments. Our phone consultants were overrun with so many calls that we had to quickly triple the number of people to handle them. Three other departments jumped right in to help, and for the next two hours everyone became a consultant.

Later that day I walked by one of the other departments and saw someone quickly stuffing envelopes and still answering some of the residual calls coming in from that promotion. Between calls, she told me that she had to finish these by two o'clock to make her deadline. I quickly sat down and helped her stuff the remaining envelopes. Someone might question why a CEO would stuff envelopes, and I would reply, "For the same reason she was helping the other department answer calls. She set the example, and in this case I followed because the right example extends beyond titles and beyond departments."

We all lead by example, whether the tasks are large or small.

Nowhere is the need to earn leadership respect more prevalent than in the military. When they pin the bars on each shoulder of the new lieutenant, that green officer has just been given rank, but from that moment on the troops will expect that officer to earn it. James M. Kouzes and Barry Z. Posner, authors of *The Leadership Challenge*, write that "titles are granted, but it's your behavior that wins you respect."[5] You will garner more respect leading by example than you ever will by just demanding it. People within an organization will rarely walk a path they have not seen their leaders walk first. Albert Schweitzer believed that "example is not the main thing in influencing others, it is the only thing."

4. Pull with Determination

During the sixth century BC, China was ruled by a merciless feudal system. Leadership was usually equated with pride and brutality until a royal court archivist named Lao Tzu redefined it with his work, the *Tao Te Ching*. He illustrated the importance of humility coupled with the power of determination by using the analogy of water, when he wrote, "Nothing in the world is softer or weaker than water yet nothing is better at overcoming the hard and strong." One look at the Grand Canyon and you understand this principle. You probably remember when excessive rain caused flood waters to permanently change the path of the Mississippi River through a couple of states in the mid-1990s. Water is not hard, but when applied in a steady and focused manner, it can be an exponentially powerful force.

Force is probably not the option you should choose for how you manage your team, but determination can have a subtle and compelling effect. Leading is not easy, and you must sometimes reach down deep to collect your strength before stepping out in pursuit of your vision. Many times you step alone, and the last thing to move when you pull the

Slinky® Dog is the tail. It stays put even when every other part of the Slinky® Dog is rushing forward, and only at that last minute does it spring forward. By position alone it fights against the move. Remember, the people who fight the pull are the ones who need it the most.

There is no steadfast rule for how long it takes people to adopt the vision. Who knows when the rest of your organization will catch up to you? Remain committed regardless

> Remember, the people who fight the pull are the ones who need it the most.

of how long it takes. If your vision is true, then hold firm—they are coming. Some look to your staying power for inspiration. Late adopters are in every organization; don't sweat it. Just be determined to help them move forward by showing them the benefits of doing so.

Determination also requires stamina, because after your people catch up, you must be ready to stretch them again if you are to continue moving forward. This repeated movement of stretching and catching up requires the leader to have stamina. When you pull the organization forward, it requires a lot of your energy. For the back to catch up to you requires energy from them as well. Therefore, while you as the leader should be prepared for the next move forward, when the back does catch up, there should be time for them to rest while they await your next move. Leaders get their rest during their planning mode, waiting for the back to catch up.

In essence, at any given moment some part of the organization is moving while simultaneously another part of the organization is resting. For this reason, you cannot be constantly pulling, or both you and the organization will remain in chaos, facing burnout.

Problems with the Pull

There is a danger with the springing action of the Slinky® Dog. Hooke's Law also states that if the stress applied to a body goes beyond a certain value (known as the elastic limit), the body will not return to its original state once the stress is removed. This means if you pull too far ahead, overstretching for too long, the back end will loose the ability to return to its place near the front, thus hindering its ability to move at all. A severe pull in the wrong direction can crimp the spring, leaving permanent damage.

While a good leader would never deliberately harm the organization, unintentional damage may be inflicted by problematic pulls. Be watchful for these four potential problems with the visionary pull.

1. Not Pulling Far Enough

If you sense you are not making the progress you desire, it could be that you are not pulling far enough. When you don't sufficiently challenge your organization to make a substantial move forward, you limit its potential. When you stretch people with strong vision, you are telling them you have confidence in them, their talents, and their abilities to make it happen.

You will only move as far ahead as you are willing to pull. Little tugs can equal baby steps, while firm pulls translate into giant leaps forward. A racecar drafting off the car it is following is similar to the slight pull of a Slinky® Dog that causes the back end to exert very little energy to keep up with those in front. This drafting effect makes them feel inconvenienced or like non-contributors to the overall success of the organization. When you cast vision, make sure to cast it far enough to help the team know they are going to be changing a few things in order to reach this goal. It requires a bit of stress to build up enough energy for that Slinky® Dog to lunge forward. Find the goal and stretch to get there by pulling far enough.

2. Pulling Too Far

Pulling too far is the greatest danger facing leaders who understand and live by vision. Running so far ahead is commonplace for the dreamer who sees where the organization needs to go and cannot wait to get there. Pulling too far happens when a leader is not willing to reach his vision a little at a time. You've probably seen a Slinky® Dog that has been over-extended—it sags in the middle, the spring has gaps in it, and it won't move straight; in fact, it looks used up. That is exactly what happens when a leader pulls too far.

Overextending the organization occurs when late adopters do not want to be moved. Winston Churchill explained, "Do you know why the nose of a bull dog is sloped backwards? So it can keep on breathing without ever letting go." Stubbornness comes in all shapes and sizes. The Churchill quote may refer to those being stubborn and not wanting to move, but it may also refer to leaders who are adamant about moving too quickly.

3. Pulling Too Soon

Not only can you stretch your team too far, but you can also stretch them too soon. Knowing when to pull is the difference between good morale and a mutiny. Leaders have a different outlook on pace and change. Many times you can't move fast enough and it seems as though you are crawling. When you think you are crawling, others think you are traveling at sonic speed. It is all perspective, but a person's perspective is his reality.

Give the organization time to catch up and breathe before launching out again into another major stride. Management has two major steps that few leaders are able to manage together. One is to pioneer new frontiers, and the other is to settle the territory you have just conquered. If you do not take time to organize the new ground, you may lose it down the road. Be patient by stretching and allowing the back of the Slinky® Dog to catch up. The front is the conquering part of the organization, and the back is the settling part. You need both.

4. Pulling from the Wrong End

How many times have you been trying to make progress only to find someone in the organization pulling the dog by the tail? In the worst cases, that someone is the leader. Unfortunately we have all seen a leader pulling an organization from the wrong end by moving without a direction or acting without a cooperative plan. Not only is no progress made, but previously conquered ground is lost. In an effort to get going in the right direction, the leader mistakenly pulls from the wrong end. If you're not pulling the Slinky® Dog in the right direction, then you are going nowhere.

Pull, and Then Be Patient

You must move before anyone follows you. If you are waiting for your team to move, then maybe you have not stretched them far enough. But do not get too far ahead. Remember what Franklin D. Roosevelt said: "A good leader can't get too far ahead of his followers." Vision pulls an institution or team forward and then patiently waits for the back end to catch up.

To get moving you must first find the string. Each organization has a different string. Each individual has a unique point of contact. What is the motivating factor of those you are leading: Profit? Efficiency? Reward? Success? Recognition? Purpose? It is your job as the leader to find the string, pull it, and then be patient.

3 Play-Doh®

Motivations for inventing toys vary as much as the toys themselves. For some it is money, for some it is fame, and for some it is just plain fun. Play-Doh® compound is unique because it was educationally motivated. With all that creativity in a can, it is no wonder a teacher discovered Play-Doh® compound.

Her name was Kay Zufall, and she operated a neighborhood nursery school in Dover, New Jersey. It was Christmastime 1954, and Kay was looking for creative ways for the children to decorate their classroom. She read that people were shaping ornaments out of a claylike wallpaper cleaner and then painting them after they hardened, so she tried it. The kids loved playing with the soft clay so much that she called her brother-in-law (the owner of the failing Kutol wallpaper cleaner company) and told him that his compound made for a great toy. He flew to New Jersey to talk to her and was so impressed with her idea that he immediately went back to Cincinnati, took the detergents out of the mix, and introduced Kutol's Rainbow Modeling Compound to the world. Kay later suggested a more child-friendly name: Play-Doh® compound.

Since then more than a billion pounds of Play-Doh® compound have been manufactured. That's enough Play-Doh® compound to roll out a "snake" that would reach around the earth about three times. Every year Hasbro produces ninety-five million cans, in twenty-one colors, sold in seventy-five countries around the world.

But what makes Play-Doh® compound such a great toy? If you said, "Because it's delicious," you are not alone. Kids have probably eaten more Play-Doh® compound than glue and crayons combined. Thankfully, it is nontoxic. Next—remember that unforgettable smell? Even today one whiff takes you right back to kindergarten. That distinct smell is so popular that it was bottled as a perfume in honor of its fiftieth anniversary in 2006. Then there is the texture—soft and smooth, moist but not sticky—the perfect combination of firm and squishy. Of all the things that make Play-Doh® compound great, perhaps the best one is its unlimited potential to be shaped.

○   ○   ○

Like Play-Doh® compound, leaders resemble whatever makes an impression on them. What ideas, values, or people shape you right now? The mold you choose will make the difference in the person you become. Shaping leaders happens in both positive and negative ways. Molding should be intentional, so that *you* choose what influences you.

Play-Doh® People

Being a Play-Doh® person does not mean you are weak, gullible, or even wishy-washy, but rather that you have determined to be molded in positive ways that are essential to their development. Succeeding comes from intentionally choosing who and what shapes you, and one valuable component of success is having mentors to guide and encourage you. Never underestimate the value of the right mentor in your life.

> Succeeding comes from intentionally choosing who and what shapes you.

Denzel Washington believes in the power of mentoring. In his book *A Hand to Guide Me*, the Academy Award winner compiled the stories of seventy-three successful individuals who have credited their mentors with much of their success. He writes, "Show me a successful individual and I'll show you someone who didn't want for positive influences in his or her life."[1] On opposite extremes, you can take a trip to most any correctional facility and find story after story of blaming others. Blame usually means that people have allowed negative influences or influencers to mold their bad decisions.

While there are volumes written on being a mentor, it's

harder to find books about how to be mentored or the qualities of one being mentored. Everyone needs a mentor, but few of us really understand how to find one. Play-Doh® compound can help you understand how to put yourself in a position to be shaped and mentored.

Play-Doh® Principles

Think about this: the fun of Play-Doh® compound depends upon its moldability. If it loses that, it hardens and you throw it away. What qualities make it pliable, adaptable, and impressionable? You must learn these lessons in order to be mentored.

Play-Doh® People Are Shaped Because They Are Open

Go to any children's classroom and you'll see rows of little yellow cans sitting on the shelf. Pretty? Yes. Fun? Not until opened. The same is true with people. To be mentorable you must be open. Open to change and being changed. You must open yourself to advice, to new ideas, and to different habits. It is never too late to open yourself up to the process.

As great a golfer as Tiger Woods is, he remains open to coaching and learning. He admitted as much when he said, "No matter how good you get you can always get better, and that's the exciting part." Children and teenagers are easily shaped because of their desire to be like others. They play backyard ball just like their heroes. They imitate and dress like them. The posters hanging in their rooms show the people who shape a large portion of their adolescence. While posters may not hang in your offices today, you still imitate people in your habits, preferences, management style, and business beliefs. Are you consciously choosing who you imitate, or are you simply following whoever happens to be in your environment?

Play-Doh® People Are Shaped Because of Their Character

Play-Doh® compound is durable. Think about it—you can squeeze it, mash it, squash it, pull it, roll it, or cut it, and it remains Play-Doh® compound. Why? Because of its ingredients. Basically, Play-Doh® compound is a combination of water, starch, salt, lubricant, and preservative. These exact ingredients allow the substance to have consistent integrity. There are three ingredients that you must possess to be consistently mentored.

The first ingredient is humility. Growing leaders must admit that they do not have all the answers. They must honestly see their need for more knowledge. Growing leaders must know their capabilities and weaknesses. If you cannot recognize your own deficiency, you will never submit yourself to be mentored. For improvement to take place, you must admit the need to improve, and that requires a humble spirit. Often pride prevents many average leaders from becoming great ones. When you see yourself realistically, then being humble is not admitting weakness but admitting there is room for development.

The great western writer Louis L'Amour loved learning so much he entitled his autobiography *Education of a Wandering Man*. In his novel *To the Far Blue Mountains*, he phrases the need for learning this way: "The more one learns, the more he understands his ignorance."[2] Applying an honest assessment gives you an inventory of not only your talents and strengths but, inversely, your weaknesses. By categorizing these, you can begin seeking a mentor for specific areas. Only then can you be coached or mentored to new heights.

The second ingredient is teachability. *Teachability* may not be in your spellchecker, but it better be in your vocabulary. Teachability is the willingness to learn. The person who cannot be taught anything is useless to an organization. The leader who cannot learn new lessons will have nothing of long-term value to

> *Teachability* may not be in your spellchecker, but it better be in your vocabulary.

teach his followers. You cannot model what is not there. You may remember a clever saying that is very applicable here: "If your output is more than your input, then your upkeep will be your downfall."

It was John F. Kennedy's experience that "leadership and learning are indispensable to each other." Approach every day looking to learn from someone or some event. Knowledge can come from colleagues, the news, books, or your family. The key is to be teachable.

The third ingredient is desire. You might assume that humility combined with teachability produces mentorability. You would be mistaken, because those two ingredients do not automatically instill the desire to improve in a certain area. You may be humble and teachable and yet weak in math or accounting, and refuse to seek help or growth in this area. You must desire to be positively shaped in deficient areas. It will never happen accidentally. Winston Churchill said, "The most important thing about education is appetite."

Appetite, passion, desire—if they are missing, you will never find the mold your life needs. A hunger to learn is the beginning of knowledge. If you are an eager learner, you will quickly become a teacher of others. If you lack that desire to learn, however, ultimately you won't be able to teach anyone. Tackle life every day with a passion to learn. If you are looking for it, it will come. Alertness and expectancy create an environment of learning. Only then will you approach life as a series of lessons.

Play-Doh® People Are Shaped by Molds

Once you have the ingredients of humility, teachability, and desire, then you select the mold. The mold you choose determines the final product. Making yourself a better leader means choosing molds such as people or books, or just listening.

The Mentoring Mold of People

Who are the mentors in your life? People often think of business leaders, parents, drill sergeants, coaches, teachers, previous managers, or pastors. Each would make a great mentor if he or she has your best interest in mind. Some people mentor without the intent of being looked at as a mentor; they just naturally shape our lives. You may need to ask one of these people to address a specific area of your life.

You may be wondering how to start this process. Go to the person and say something like, "You have already taught me so much, and since you have my best interest at heart, I'm asking you to speak into my life in this certain area. I would appreciate any thoughts you have and will not take it personally. I will always receive your words as an evaluation to help me become better." It truly is this simple; just invite the person's advice, impressions, and suggestions into your life. You are not agreeing to do everything he or she says. You are simply asking for that person's input in your life.

Look beyond the obvious choices from the list above and consider other potential mentors. Retired people in your field have life experiences beyond current technology that may be very valuable. Invite competitors to lunch and see what passing remarks they offer, knowing many great lessons can occur during small talk. Talk with your managers and pick their brains. Asking their advice will surprise them, and their answers could surprise you. People who may not even be in your field can shape your character.

The next time you're in a meeting, take a can of Play-Doh® compound, open it up, and start squeezing and shaping it. It will be a subconscious distraction that may energize your creativity. When you set it down, look at the material very closely, and one striking result will be your fingerprints all over the surface. When you allow people to mentor you, they, too, will leave their fingerprints.

But you should never confuse mentoring with duplication. Good mentors do not wish to duplicate themselves. They simply want to invest in another's life by helping them reach greater heights than they could have reached alone. If you cannot keep and enhance your own personality while being mentored, then you may need to find a new mentor.

The Mentoring Mold of Books

At a large publishers conference, NBA executive Pat Williams, a sought-after motivational speaker and author, spoke. Being a senior VP, he talked about the workout facility for the players, explaining that Nautilus makes exercise equipment for virtually every muscle in the human body.

He then paused and said, "They have yet to come up with a single piece of equipment to work out the human mind." He suggested that reading a book would take you places, teach you, and ultimately provide a workout for the mind. He also said that "the average person after leaving high school or college reads less than one non-fiction book the rest of their life." He concluded by suggesting that reading three books on any given topic, then, would make one an expert in that field.

Reading books mentors a person in very specific ways. You can gain expertise from people you may never have the chance to meet. Books will mold and shape your professional and personal life. If your excuse is you are too busy, consider audio books for all that windshield time. One thing Ron knows about is windshield time. Here is how he summarizes his philosophy of audio books:

> While working in central Florida, I spent a considerable amount of time on the road. Realizing that most radio is bubble gum for the ears, I always felt that this time could be better utilized. I began to check out audio books from the local library or rent them from Cracker Barrel. The result was that I would listen to about three books a week, which translates into learning from over 150 authors a year. This maximized my time and shaped my professional development.

When it comes to books, remember the words of Mark Twain: "The man who does not read books has no advantage over the man who can't read them."[3]

The Mentoring Mold of Listening

Molding occurs by listening more than talking. Listening provides people an opportunity to mentor without ever officially bestowing the title upon them. Find places where conversations can be joined and then just sit back and take it all in while resisting the need to steer the conversation. Listen and ask questions that go beyond surface-level communication. Probe people's rationale. Ask what options they pondered and how they settled on the decision. Ask what they might do differently. Ask in order to understand their thoughts and emotions.

Early in our professional careers, we had the honor of meeting Dr. Melvin Maxwell, father of leadership expert John Maxwell. He was conducting a conference, and we were privileged enough to get some personal time with him. As expected, he offered some very practical advice. He told us that as we travel we should seek out leaders in our profession and ask them for just five minutes of their time, knowing that most will not agree to more. He encouraged us to prepare questions ahead of time and interview them with the sole purpose of being mentored for five minutes. After doing this several times, each of us has found that most of the time those five minutes were extended further when the leader saw that we really cared about learning from him or her. Whom could you listen to and learn from today?

Play-Doh® People Are Shaped When They Are Fresh

Any kid will tell you that if Play-Doh® compound is not fresh, it's no fun at all. Freshness doesn't happen by accident. Keep your mind fresh and impressionable by staying in the right environment and, like Play-Doh® compound, in the right hands. You stay fresh by making an effort to grow. McDonald's founder Ray Kroc knew the importance of this truth. He taught his employees, "As long as you're green, you're growing. As soon as you're ripe, you start to rot."[4] Freshness also comes from frequent use. A leader, at any stage, cannot afford to stop being shaped. Play-Doh® compound that cannot be shaped will have certain problems, much like people who refuse to be mentored.

Play-Doh® Problems

Michael has had a few Play-Doh® problems with his children. Here is one you might relate to:

One Saturday my wife was speaking at a conference out of town, and I was watching our three sons who were four, five, and six at that time. The events that would follow will be forever referred to in our household as "The Play-Doh® compound incident."

I asked the boys what they wanted to play with, and they unanimously said, "Play-Doh." I opened a new three-pack and set it out on the kitchen table. Leaving them content, I went into the other room to watch football. About twenty minutes later I returned to find the three different colors had been fused together into a giant rainbow ball with an assortment of foreign objects throughout. I was determined to find out what was in there, so I dissected the sphere like a bad CSI agent.

First, there was salt and pepper that they had added while making the Play-Doh® compound into a pizza. Next, there were several dozen human hairs that they each denied having contributed, but the colored residue on their foreheads told a different story. Then there were ladybugs they collected by rolling the ball across the front porch. The remainder of my findings included seven LEGO® bricks, two Matchbox cars, and a nickel.

Having successfully concluded my investigation, I declared Play-Doh® compound time over, and while putting the mixed-up dough into the three cans, I found about half a can missing. I asked the boys where the rest of the Play-Doh® compound was, but they denied any such knowledge. That mystery was solved the next morning when my bread wouldn't go into the toaster.

Needless to say, those cans of Play-Doh® compound were never used again. Three things, specifically, can happen to Play-Doh® compound to cause it to lose its ability to be shaped. These three can parallel what happens to a life that fails to be mentored.

1. You Can't Unmix It

As noted in the giant rainbow ball mentioned in the story above, blending colors presents one major problem—you can't unmix them. As interesting as it looks, it is stuck that way. You cannot separate the colors. At this point, it can only become more mixed up. The lesson is this: some traits are nearly impossible to unlearn. Losing bad habits is harder than gaining good ones. We unintentionally catch poor behavior from unexpected sources. Be on your guard to prevent mixing traits that should not be in your professional, personal, moral, or ethical fiber. Identify those traits in your life that should not be in the mix, and unlike Play-Doh® compound, you can with serious determination unmix bad habits and behavior.

2. If It Is Not Kept Fresh, It Will Harden

Prolonged exposure to an unhealthy environment will cause irreparable damage to Play-Doh® compound. In the world around you, the status quo is not conducive to staying fresh. Hurting others in order to get ahead creates callousness in business. Never let someone fool you into believing leaders must be ruthless at all costs. Stepping on or over people will harden your exterior and prevent the closeness necessary for mentoring. When people become so business-hardened that they cannot be touched by others, then their teachability, humility, and desire are replaced by self-centeredness and self-preservation. Unguarded, we will be resistant to new ideas and subsequently uninterested in growth. Be careful of your surroundings. Be pliable and stay fresh so that you will remain impressionable.

3. If It Hardens, It Will Crack

After Play-Doh® compound hardens, cracks begin to appear. Cracks showing in the exterior are a symptom of a much deeper problem. You will not be able to grow for having to deal with the cracks. The integrity of your ingredients has been compromised. Replacing teachability with hard exteriors denies you many growth opportunities. Giant sequoia trees remind you that strength is not in rigidity but in the gentle ability to bend with circumstances without being uprooted. Leaders must be flexible while never sacrificing their root values.

○   ○   ○

A successful leader knows the shaping process never stops. Real Play-Doh® people will practice the principles and avoid the problems. Analyzing those who have influenced your life is a good first step. Ron remembers some of the mentors who have molded him:

I have been fortunate to have been mentored by some ordinary people with outstanding results. A kindergarten teacher who began to shape my independence; a fourth-grade teacher who taught me to write in cursive; a sixth-grade teacher who had very high standards; my parents, who always expected my very best; a drill sergeant who helped increase my confidence; a leader in a state organization who taught me board ethics; and several college professors who shaped my attention to current events, political leanings, my marriage, and my values. I still have many people who continue to challenge me and speak into my life, making me a better person. I am quite sure your list is very similar to this one, but the question is—who is shaping your life today?

4 Yo-Yo

CREATIVITY
It Only Happens When You Let Go

At the height of the Watergate scandal, President Richard Nixon went onstage at the Grand Ole Opry in Nashville, Tennessee. He didn't sing, give a speech, or tell jokes. Instead he played with a yo-yo. The yo-yo belonged to Roy Acuff, who had incorporated yo-yo tricks into his act for years. After the show, the president signed the toy and presented it to the singer. Years later that item sold at the Acuff estate auction for $16,029, making it the world-record price ever paid for a yo-yo.

Historians agree that the yo-yo is one of the oldest toys in history. However, they disagree on its point of origin because it seems to have appeared in multiple sites at various times. Similar toys have been documented in China around 1000 BC and then five hundred years later in Greece. The most unusual theory is that it evolved from a sixteenth-century weapon used by hunters in the Philippines. The first public mention of the toy in North America was in the patent obtained by

James L. Haven and Charles Hettrick in 1866. Throughout history this toy has been known by many names, but an article in a 1916 issue of the *Scientific American Supplement* gave detailed instructions on how to make this "Filipino toy" and called it by its island name, the "yo-yo."

The modern yo-yo craze began in 1928, when Pedro Flores trademarked the name "yo-yo" and began manufacturing thousands of units per day. Two years later, Flores sold his business to Donald F. Duncan, a toy marketing genius. His new "Duncan Yo-Yo" would dominate the market for the next thirty-five years, accounting for up to 85 percent of the yo-yos sold in the United States, including an astonishing forty-five million in 1962.

Duncan would say that the success of the yo-yo could be attributed to his annual nationwide yo-yo contests more than anything else. At these events, the average person could recognize the excitement and creative potential of this toy. Today people of all ages still love the yo-yo because of its simplicity and the nearly limitless possibilities.

○   ○   ○

Remember the first time you played with a yo-yo? Step back in time with Michael when he received his first yo-yo:

> I got my first Duncan Butterfly yo-yo when I was eleven after seeing a professional yo-yo demonstrator at the mall

and deciding that there could be no greater job in the world than this. That first day I tried to do all the tricks I had seen him perform: Walk the Dog, Around the World, and Rock the Cradle, to name a few. The only problem was that I kept hitting myself in the head. The more I tried, the more tangled and dangerous the toy became. After a week, I had numerous knots in the string (not to mention my head), so I cut the string shorter. This only made the yo-yo more unmanageable. The good news was it was too short to hit me in the head anymore, but the bad news was the string was now too short to do any tricks. So for weeks I just carried it around in my pocket until finally retiring it to the shelf. And there it stayed until I found it while helping my parents move, some twenty-eight years later.

Creativity is very much like a yo-yo. It remains dormant until it is released. Good ideas are a commodity. Since many organizations will live or die based on the stream of ideas they can produce, creativity is the fuel for growth and opportunity. Many times creative solutions are better than expensive ones. Creativity can be the fuel that propels your business. Ideas, enhancements, improvements, developments, inspirations, and initiatives not only keep your business on the cutting edge but also ensure viability. This chapter shows the value of creativity and creative people. It will spark your creative genius, even if your tank seems to stay on empty.

According to Michael Michalko, one of the world's leading experts in the field of creativity, creative people are simply those who come up with more ideas in a shorter space of time. Some people think that this only happens to certain people or personalities. But the truth is everyone has the ability to be more creative when the conditions are right. You can learn to be more inventive, more ingenious, and more imaginative than you ever thought possible. You can also help others to release their creative side. Remember, good leaders don't necessarily need to be exceedingly creative to be successful, but they must surround themselves with people who are. The yo-yo teaches you how to equip yourself and others to be more innovative by developing the kind of environment and processes that generate valuable ideas.

> Remember, good leaders don't necessarily need to be exceedingly creative to be successful, but they must surround themselves with people who are.

Organizations often underestimate the value of creative people. Creative people connect the dots when others don't. They make observations about products, services, or presentations that are obvious to them but others miss. They see where modifications can be made or how to mix one idea with another, resulting in effective cross-pollination. Simply put, creativity creates opportunities.

The Purpose-Driven Yo-Yo

Think about how a yo-yo would spin if the axle were off-center. The yo-yo would wobble down the string absent the momentum needed to return back to your hand. The same is true of creativity. It is best when it has a central goal or problem to solve around which all the discussion should revolve. Want to see your team get creative? Put them in a room and tell them to come up with one hundred ways (with money as no object) to make your product or service better.

Make Creativity Attractive

Make creativity so attractive that achieving it benefits the whole team and gets them talking. Give them creative topics to discuss, and it will create ownership within their area and allow them to think creatively about the whole organization. People need a central purpose for their ideas and discussions. That is why water-cooler talk is so popular—it is based upon a pop culture event, a ballgame, or another office member. Admiral Hyman Rickover once said, "Great minds discuss ideas, average minds discuss events, small minds discuss people." The most attractive thing about creativity is that with it you gain influence and affect administrative decisions regardless of your title.

Give Creativity a Direction

Creativity requires a direction. This is largely due to the proven cliché "necessity is the mother of invention." Invention is creativity that solves problems. Just as the yo-yo's inertia and course is provided by the throw, people need guidance and purpose for their imagination. David Allen, best-selling author of *Getting Things Done: The Art of Stress-Free Productivity*, says it is "hard to be fully creative without structure and constraint."[1] He illustrates this with a futile effort to paint without a canvas. It is a leader's responsibility to guarantee fluency and flexibility of thought with clear expectations.

Many people talk about being creative but seldom make the jump to creativity because they are unsure how to begin. Since there is no prescribed route to follow, astrophysicist Stephen Hawking says forming new ideas requires you to take "the intuitive leap." Direct your team's creativity and help them make that leap to solve your organization's problems.

The Requirements of Creativity

There are four requirements for the yo-yo to work, and those same requirements mirror the creative process: releasing, revolving, returning, and rewinding. Follow these creative absolutes and you will unleash your creative potential and the creative potential of those you lead.

1. Creativity Requires Releasing

With all of its potential, a yo-yo is simply a paperweight until you let it go. It won't work if you just hold it. Only when you let go will it do what it was designed to do, and that is to spin. Letting go is the removal of constrictions. Creativity is often squashed by restrictive boundaries, unnecessary policies, and lack of opportunities. While it sounds overly simplified, the process demands that you first have to let go. Walt Disney, an icon of creativity, said, "The way to get started is to quit talking and begin doing." Make the choice to be creative.

Disney often used the term *Imagineer* to describe a very creative person. Your organization could benefit from you being an Imagineer like Walt. "Walt Disney was a visionary and a futurist. And what is a futurist? . . . A futurist is a planner and a doer. Futurists look at trends and innovations. They look for patterns of change. They then act. Futurists don't just predict the future. They make the future happen."[2]

When you do actually "let go," you make available a variety of freedoms. *The first of these is the freedom to think.* This wide-open approach is crucial for the mind to encounter something new. It is in that free space that you find the liberty to dream. If you're imprisoned by the day-to-day stress of running your organization, you will find little room for innovative thoughts. Never underestimate the value of freeing up creative time. Your organization's future will suffer when you're too constrained to dream. Plan creative time in your calendar just as if it were a real appointment. Always have something to record your ideas: a legal pad, Post-it notes, or a voice recorder. If you have creative thoughts while you are driving, you can record them on voice mail. In your mind, replay your day on your drive home. Think through what was accomplished, what is pending, what was left undone, and how you could have improved the day. You can also spend your drive time on the phone bouncing ideas off of people who can give you solid feedback. Create the time to think.

Another essential freedom is the freedom to explore. Most innovation today comes from looking at the old in new ways. Exploration forces you to study all the angles. It causes you to search for new possibilities. Renowned psychoanalyst Erich Fromm stated, "Creativity requires the courage to let go of certainties." This only happens when you are willing to leave your current mind-set. *If you hold on too tightly, your perspective narrows and you exchange creativity for comfort.* Allow those around you to explore. Even Walt Disney recognized the value of his team exploring possibilities, so he ensured they had a work environment that sparked creativity.

Letting go to explore works best with an attitude of trust. Trust is expecting that the method will help you accomplish the goal. As a leader, you may not live consistently outside the box, but you need people around you who do. And to

> As a leader, you may not live consistently outside the box, but you need people around you who do.

maximize creativity, a leader needs to trust those who do think outside the box.

The most important creative freedom by far is the freedom to fail. How many people ever get the yo-yo trick right on the first try? Does your team have permission to fail while being creative? If so, you are cultivating a winning team of creators. But if they fear your rebuke because of a failed attempt at something new, they may revert back to not risking anything at all. Just remember, the consequences of failing are small compared to the consequences of not trying at all. H. Jackson Brown, best-selling author, said it best: "You pay the price for getting stronger. You pay the price for getting faster. You pay the price for jumping higher. [But also] you pay the price for staying just the same."[3] Do not be afraid of failing.

Here is an exercise in creativity Ron uses that may produce results in your organization:

I like to use managers' meetings for training and development. Many times meetings can become calendar synchronizers and newsletter updates, most of which can be e-mailed. When you get people together, make it worth their time. Have a plan for training and spend at least fifteen minutes of the meeting accomplishing this task. I usually pick a book to work through, and we discuss a chapter each meeting and how principles from that book can improve our organization.

I wanted to take the development to a new level, and yet time was valuable, so I devised a system of creatively allowing every manager a chance to throw an idea on the table, with brief context, to let the other managers further develop the idea through feedback. The process has been named I^3— Immediate Idea Infusion.

There are three parameters to using this effectively. (1) Idea—Each manager gets one minute to introduce an idea they want feedback on from other managers relating to strengthening a department, organization, or a person. In short, it is about growing. (2) Immediate—Collectively they get two minutes to speak to this idea; comments should not be personal, should not leave dead air, and should use short, rapid thoughts. During the two minutes, the first is used for the pros of the idea and the second is for cons. Never kill an idea with cons before the pros show the potential. (3) Infusion—Infusion is the result of multiple ideas being exchanged and discussed. This always results in better understanding between managers and departments, and it opens new channels of dialogue outside the sessions. It strengthens and brings us closer together based upon the "iron sharpening iron" principle. This has added about thirty minutes to the meetings, but you should see the plethora of ideas generated in that half hour.

2. Creativity Requires Revolving

Once a yo-yo is released, it begins the revolution process. In other words, it spins. The American Yo-Yo Association world record for allowing a yo-yo to spin or "sleep" at the end of the string and still return was set by Rick Wyatt at thirteen minutes and five seconds. What would happen if you were to release a yo-yo and it didn't spin? It would travel to the end of its string and stay there. Without the revolving it lacks the motivating inertia needed to travel its path. Like the yo-yo, creativity cannot be rushed either—it needs time to revolve and gain the necessary momentum to return with creativity in hand. In her book *The Creative Habit: Learn It and Use It for Life*, Twyla Tharp writes that Mozart once commented, "People err who think my art comes easily to me. I assure you dear friend, nobody has devoted so much time and thought to composition as I."[4] It takes time to think.

It also takes time to try and try again. It took Thomas Edison more than fifty thousand attempts to create the alkaline battery that we still use today. Just like Edison, you will seldom get it exactly right on the first attempt. There are no substitutes for time—it is the vehicle of determination. Edison's continued creativity shows the value of persistent revolving to reach one's goal.

Without a doubt, one of the most innovative companies in the last century is Apple Corporation. Its CEO, Steve Jobs, says, "You cannot mandate productivity," but what you must do is "provide the tools to let people become their best." Before you lament the lack of ideas coming across your desk, find out if those around you understand what is needed and if they have the tools to produce it. Those who fail to provide such tools will find their creativity well running dry. You need time to hash out ideas—revolving over and over—floating the impossible to see if it can become a reality.

The last component of revolving is confidence. As Dr. Wayne Dyer maintains, "Creativity means believing you have greatness." Truly creative people trust their pioneering skills. Pat Williams describes Walt Disney's ability to see tomorrow: "Sometimes there's a fine line between a visionary genius and a total looney."[5] Have the confidence to float silly ideas to show your team that there are no boundaries around your creativity. There is no substitute to knowing that you can generate a great idea. Be courageous enough to think the unusual no matter how goofy it may sound. Great ideas come bunched with the silly ones.

> Great ideas come bunched with the silly ones.

Think of all the imaginative ideas that drew criticism. Communications expert Everett M. Rogers suggests,

When five percent of society accepts an idea, it becomes imbedded in the population. When 20 percent agrees, it's unstoppable. Even the unstoppable gets criticized.

"You can't put a crocodile on a shirt and replace the pocket. Nobody will buy it."

"You want to sell me a chicken recipe? You'll never get this idea off the ground, Colonel Sanders."

"I'm sorry, but your *Gone With the Wind* manuscript will have little public appeal."

"Watches with no hands? You're crazy!"

The history books are full of people who realized creativity begins with destroying perceived limitations and remaining untouched by criticism.[6]

You are never more open to criticism than the very moment you vocalize a new concept. But the risk is worth the reward of birthing a solution to what seems impossible. Start slow and let it spin until the right idea comes. Revolving is the state of creativity that manifests itself in a myriad of ways, such as inventing through failure, dreaming the impossible, and suggesting the absurd.

> You are never more open to criticism than the very moment you vocalize a new concept.

3. Creativity Requires Returning

Throwing a yo-yo is only half the fun. The object of the toy's motion is not complete until the yo-yo spins back up the string into your hand. An innovative concept becomes functional only when it has returned and finally is put to the test. Charles Douglas Jackson, a special assistant to President Eisenhower, put it best when he said, "Great ideas need landing gear as well as wings." The return means creativity comes back to positively affect the organization. For instance, in brainstorming you must have wide parameters, but you should still maintain parameters.

Your most creative idea is useless if it exists only in the arena of theory. When you generate ideas, they should have practical application to the organization. Imagine you are in the huddle with your favorite football team as great offensive plays are dreamed up and discussed. The confident quarterback believes his plans will result in a touchdown and inevitably end up in the ESPN highlight reels. You stand and wait for the players to break from the huddle, but they never do. All they do is talk. After a few delay-of-game penalties, you realize that all this talk with no action is moving you backward. Does that sound familiar? The greatest play ever designed is of no use if it's not tested on the field. People can be creative and come up with incredible concepts that have no value to growing the organization. This is why the return is so important to the creative process: because it provides accountability and closure.

As valuable as "spin-time" is, it can lead to terrible procrastination. You manage creativity by giving direction and expecting the return. If you are not time conscious, then your creativity can "spin" for days without any results, because your view of time is so very abstract. It helps to recognize that this will frustrate your time-conscious coworker. Spending only three hours on a project may seem restrictive, but for an accounting person that may seem a waste of time. As in most areas of life, your personality determines your perspective. Accountability helps you become a recognizably valued team member because firm deadlines and clear expectations provide viable and measurable goals.

Creative people hate criticism, but it is vital for the process to continue. Creative people live in their own world. While they may be protective of their work, given constructively and honestly, feedback on how their ideas must return to the organization will be welcomed. When you evaluate creative people, critique their performance but never criticize the person. Honest assessment and analysis, without personal attack, provide an objective look at the creation process. In this manner even the best ideas can improve. Use criticism as an impetus to further improve your ideas rather than abandon them. The correct type of critique communicates the value people bring while also motivating them. This transforms perceived weaknesses into valued strengths for everyone in the organization.

Do you often reward the doers or the implementers of the tasks while overlooking the creative people who set the process in motion? Most of the time creative people are not the ones who implement an idea. Providing recognition or reward concludes the return stage. Jeff Mauzy and Richard Harriman, in their book *Creativity Inc.: Building an Inventive Organization*, write that "individuals who receive little reward and support for creative work will reduce their creative efforts."[7] Never castigate someone for an idea that bombs. Many times you reward the attempt rather than the result. In celebrating creativity, you will develop an atmosphere where it can flourish.

The LEGO® principle from chapter 1 comes into play at this point, because as a leader, you should connect creative people with technical people in order to improve the quality and performance of both groups. Wouldn't your office environment feel more like a grindstone without the creative minds making it fun and exciting? They incite the pranks, crack jokes in the meetings, and often give offbeat interpretations of the office memos. But never forget, they put the attraction factor in your business.

4. Creativity Requires Rewinding

Everyone's yo-yo stops spinning at some point. Every writer, artist, strategist, architect, or designer of any type at some point hits the proverbial brick wall with no creative flow. It is then that you must rewind the string before letting it go again.

Creativity requires energy, and you only have a finite amount. No gauge tells you when your source runs low, so develop the habit of proactively renewing your mind and your ideas. You know you have reached a creative roadblock when the volume of the ideas you generate decreases or the quality falls flat. Rewinding your string regenerates your creativity. So how do you rewind the string and boost your creativity when you can't seem to squeeze out one more idea?

Get an appropriate amount of rest, and do not underestimate the clarity it gives the mind. Consider role swapping to see a different perspective and what the other person might do. Play your favorite music. Have a method to capture your thoughts. Use lots of Post-it notes. Use a mind-mapping technique so that ideas do not have to be linear. Crank out as many possibilities as you can in a set time, put them aside, and then come back later to explore them individually.

When working with groups, a poorly worded question will place a ceiling on the discussion. Shape your questions with few parameters to promote many answers. Encourage observation from different angles. This is how Velcro came into being—through a closer observation of those Burdock Seeds that stick to your pants and shoelaces. Break your routines for a day or two by doing something you don't normally do, such as riding a bike, driving to work by a different route, ordering something you have never eaten, reading a different genre of book, or taking a walk at lunch. Associate with diverse individuals and listen to their experiences. Each new relationship can bring out an untapped segment of your personality. These are just a few ideas to boost your creativity. There are many good books devoted entirely to creativity if you want to explore more details in this area.

The obvious time to stop and rewind your creative force is after a failure. Don't give up; rather back away and temporarily remove yourself from the situation. Henry Ford explained why it is beneficial to rewind that string when he said, "Failure is the opportunity to begin again more intelligently." When you are ready to return, approach the problem from a different place or perspective.

The not-so-obvious time to reset your mind is after an exceptionally successful idea or a period of creative productivity. The reason why is best explained by Starbucks CEO Howard Schultz in his book *Pour Your Heart into It: How Starbucks Built a Company One Cup at a Time.* Schultz writes, "When you're failing, it's easy to understand the need for self-renewal. But we're seldom motivated to seek self-renewal when we're successful. When things are going well, when the fans are cheering, why change a winning formula? The simple answer is this: Because the world is changing."[8] Some creativity killers are obvious, and some are not, but all of them are detrimental.

The Killers of Creativity

Creativity killers cut your yo-yo's string. Excessive stress without the proper focus will do it every time. Lack of proper sleep and rest dulls the mind. Health problems can distract and drain one of more than just creativity. Dark or depressing rooms, noisy backgrounds, and unexpected interruptions all contribute to zapping creativity. Allowing personal attacks or criticism to get to you will distract you and derail your focus. Your schedule can kill. Allowing your creative time to be absorbed by other tasks robs you of your potential. You really must take the time or others will.

As harmful as these killers are, perhaps the most damaging killer is fear. The fall 2006 issue of *Create* magazine contains an excellent article titled "Natural Born Creativity Killers" by Bob Kodzis. In it he writes, "Fear is the Adolf Hitler of creativity killers. It is responsible for suppressing and destroying more brilliant ideas than all of the other creativity killers combined."[9] Fear paralyzes the creative process. When people lack the confidence to be creative, they will never step out of the box.

○   ○   ○

Everyone possesses creativity. Some have simply spent more time cultivating it than others. Developing creativity begins with placing yourself in creative environments. Some have held that yo-yo in their hand for so long that they forget what it's like to throw down a good idea. Just as the yo-yo goes up and down, creativity is a cyclical process as well. The best idea is seldom the first one, so grab a yo-yo and get those ideas spinning. If you do it right, then what goes down must come up. Creativity is what happens in between.

5 Mr. Potato Head®

In the 1999 hit movie *Toy Story 2*, the toys are planning to rescue Woody. And just before they leave, Mrs. Potato Head® lifts up the storage compartment in the back of Mr. Potato Head® and says, "I'm packing your extra pair of shoes, and your angry eyes, just in case." Have you ever needed a set of angry eyes only to find that you had not packed them?

The Mr. Potato Head® toy was the brainstorm of George Lerner in the late 1940s. His concept called for separate plastic facial pieces designed to be stuck into a real potato. The Mr. Potato Head® parts were originally included in boxes of cereal to promote sales. Lerner sold the product to textile manufacturers Henry and Merrill Hassenfeld, who did business as the Hassenfeld Brothers, later shortened to Hasbro. In 1952, the Mr. Potato Head® toy became the first to be advertised on network television and netted Hasbro over four million dollars in sales during its first year of production. One year later, he got some great news, when he was introduced to a Mrs. Potato Head® toy. Soon afterward, the Brother Spud and Sister Yam toys completed the Potato Head family. In the late 1950s, Hasbro changed everything by including a plastic potato-shaped body in each kit.

○   ○   ○

The Mr. Potato Head® toy can teach you so much about communicating with your face. After all, the facial features in his storage compartment are all he has to get his message across. Today, he comes complete with two arms, a nose, one pair of shoes, teeth, a mustache, two ears, a hat, a pair of eyes, a pair of glasses, and a tongue. These are of no value if unused. Remove the facial features, and all you have left is a potato. The same is true with expressionless communication.

Remember sitting on the floor with your Mr. Potato Head® toy, dumping out all of his accessories, reaching for the smile, then placing it on him? He looked so goofy you had to laugh. But soon afterward, someone turned that smile upside-down, and then everyone tried to mimic the frown he displayed. Your favorite spud could be changed to match your every mood. His expression moved from joy to anger with the simple twist of a

> No matter what your title or job description, if you work with people, communication is a vital part of what you do.

plastic mouth and a different set of eyes. You chose the face, and he wore it. That's what made him fun.

The leadership principle from the Mr. Potato Head® toy is that you must choose the right face for the right place when communicating. Why is the face so important? No matter what your title or job description, if you work with people, communication is a vital part of what you do. Family counselor and author Norman Wright defines communication as "the process of sharing yourself verbally and nonverbally in such a way that the other person can both accept and understand what you are saying."[1] In the classic book *The Art of Public Speaking*, Dale Carnegie says a speaker's "movements of the facial muscles may mean a great deal more than the movements of the hand."[2]

Most communication experts agree that up to 90 percent of your message is nonverbal—and that includes your face.

> Even when verbal language is a barrier, your face can become your primary form of communication.

Facial expressions are universal. A smile is as happy in China as it is in Connecticut. A frown is as unhappy in Argentina as it is in Alabama. Every people group around the world utilizes the face to mold the message that is coming out of the mouth. Even when verbal language is a barrier, your face can become your primary form of communication.

A stream of research points to six universal facial expressions reflecting these basic emotions: happiness, fear, sadness, surprise, anger, and disgust. Your potential, however, far exceeds those basic six. It is estimated that humans are capable of over twenty thousand unique facial expressions.[3] Getting twenty thousand expressions from a basic six requires blending.

Magazines printed in full color are actually printed using just four colors: blue, red, yellow, and black. Mixing percentages of individual colors produces a distinctly different color. Combine 56 percent blue, 33 percent yellow, and 11 percent black, and you get hunter green. Likewise, mixing the basic six emotions allows you to display greater variety of expressions. If you are disappointed, then you are mostly sad and a little angry. We can all remember the teacher wrinkling her forehead and every child in class sitting up straight, or the mom raising one eyebrow to silence a van full of soccer players. And our hearts warm when the one we most love simply smiles at us. Simple but strong expressions can be more powerful than even the spoken word.

The Right Face

There are three universal truths about the faces we wear:

1. Your Face Is a Courier of the Message

Most of the time people know what you are feeling or what you are about to say by the message you display on your face. Most books have a section before chapters begin that summarizes what the authors intend to say; it tells you what they will say before they say it. It is called the preface—because it is the face before the message. How many times has someone walked into the room and you knew what she was about to say before she even opened her mouth? That is the power of nonverbal communication.

2. Your Face Is an Extension of Your Emotions

Words convey emotion through inflection and tone. Communication becomes much more powerful when your tone is supported by your facial expressions. Not supporting your words with appropriate facial expressions is like poorly timed gestures in public speaking. They are ineffective and even distracting.

3. Your Face Is an Interpreter of Intent

When you speak to correct a behavior in someone, the seriousness of what he perceives is greatly determined by how he interprets your face. If you say, "You shouldn't have done that," while at the same time you are snickering or smiling, you are probably communicating amusement at his inappropriate behavior rather than disappointment. Genuine sincerity requires you to synchronize your facial and verbal

> The way people audibly perceive you begins with the way they visually perceive you.

expressions of communication. Paul Zucker sees facial expressions as a living language, which ultimately reveals character. What this means is the way people audibly perceive you begins with the way they visually perceive you.

Like the Mr. Potato Head® toy, leaders wear a variety of faces. While they are numerous, here are eight you should never be without.

The Eight Faces Every Leader Must Pack

1. Always Pack an Empathetic Face

Empathy is best described as a genuine understanding and appreciation of another's feelings. The people around you need to see that they are important to you. Mary Kay Cosmetics founder Mary Kay Ash said that everyone has an invisible sign around their neck that reads, "Make Me Feel Important." When people feel important, they will be empowered to do their best for you. Leaders who lack an empathic face usually find it difficult to get others to cooperate with them or their agendas.

People will trust you once they know you have genuine concern for them. Empathy connects with another person because you find common ground, whether in pain, joy, sorrow, or celebration. To share in another person's moment in an empathetic way creates a bond that goes deeper than you may ever realize. Think about those times of extreme personal loss. Be it a job, a parent, a spouse, or a child—you felt pain and loneliness in your search for answers. Your greatest aid likely came from the people you knew well but had never known they had also suffered the same loss until they shared with you while wearing an empathetic face. People want to know you care. Every day someone is looking for another person to simply listen and feel what they are feeling. When you listen, people realize they are important to you. Without saying a word, your face can express deep concern for them.

2. Always Pack a Confident Face

The battlefield is not the only place where no one wants to follow you if all they see is fear, anxiety, or vacillation. While the battlefield commander recognizes the uncertainties, the focus is on equipping the troops for victory. While people will not want to follow the face of fear, most people will work with the impossible to do the improbable if they sense the confidence of their leader!

Darting eyes or a lack of any eye contact betray a lack of confidence. Most people will interpret such an uncomfortable gaze to mean you are untrustworthy. Think about it: your credibility gone with one unmonitored glance.

Here are *three attitudes* that promote a confident face:

- **A Sense of Identity.** Be secure in who you are. People can tell if you believe in yourself. That kind of security is contagious to everyone watching you.

- **A Sense of Purpose.** Do you understand where and how you fit into the world around you? If you aren't sure, others won't be either. A confident face shows that you are comfortable with the goals before you, and you enthusiastically accept your part in them.

- **A Sense of Competence.** Competence is possessing the skills and experience to properly carry out what is expected of you. It is ability resulting from your skill, your education, your ideas, and your past successes.

3. Always Pack an Intense Face

Have you ever noticed Tiger Woods's face when he is standing over a long putt? You see an intensity that says, "This golf ball will drop in the cup." No other player currently on the PGA tour attracts more crowds around him than Tiger. Yet with thousands of eyes watching his every move, he remains intensely focused on the shot he is about to make. He proved this during the most difficult time of his career after losing his father to a long battle with cancer. Tiger came back from this tragedy by winning the British Open, the Buick Open, and the PGA Open. How did he do it? He displayed a renewed intensity even though he may have already been the most intense player on the tour. His face reflects a singular intent and an unwavering focus that few can equal.

A look of intensity translates into passionate commitment.

People can tell how close you are to quitting or conversely how far you are willing to go just by looking into your eyes. Real intensity comes from a determination to act according to plan. Intensity inspires others.

> Real intensity comes from a determination to act according to plan. Intensity inspires others.

James Kouzes and Barry Posner polled more than 7,500 managers nationwide and asked them what qualities they admired most in their leaders. Among those most mentioned were the ability to inspire and the ability to communicate with passion. Both of these can be achieved through one face—intensity.[4]

4. Always Pack an Attentive Face

It takes awareness to be attentive. An observant face demonstrates awareness. It shows an overall attentiveness of the other person and their views. It communicates value to the one speaking. If you are not aware of your surroundings, you will miss many opportunities to relate to the most important commodity in your organization: the people.

It takes respect to be attentive. Your to-do list will not get any shorter by lingering a little longer and listening to people's stories, but your interest in their story will resonate with them, helping you to understand them even better. Your attention shows you respect them. It says to them that their dialogue is as important as the rest of your day, however busy it may be.

The attentive face does not dominate the conversation or try to one-up the other person. It will not look preoccupied or bored. It shows an openness to their ideas or to their side of an issue. Ralph Waldo Emerson packed a respectful face for everyone he encountered. He said, "Every man I meet is in some way my superior, and in that I can learn of him." Respect shifts the focus to the other person.

It takes humility to be attentive. The only thing greater than being in the spotlight is when you allow it to shine on someone else. Humility is the willingness to share that spotlight with another who has earned it. Sharing the spotlight will result in dividends for your future, the future of your company, and the future success of that person. William Temple, who was archbishop of Canterbury, said that "Humility does not mean thinking less of yourself than of other people, nor does it mean having a low opinion of your own gifts. It means freedom from thinking about yourself at all." A humble face makes you approachable and results in mutually beneficial relationships with those around you.

5. Always Pack a Disappointed Face

Those around you should be able to sense your disappointment with unacceptable results before you ever open your mouth. A disappointed face is different than an angry face. An angry glare speaks of failure without possibilities of repair. Disappointment gives a person appropriate feedback with room for improvement. It says, "This work is not good enough, but there is hope."

Negative feedback should contain words that constructively build up the other person, the project, or the organization—in that order. Achieving positive growth means showing disappointment and then coaching them into success.

6. Always Pack a Happy Face

Happiness is feeling satisfied with and deriving pleasure from the circumstances around you. When you project happiness, you show approval. This is necessary when someone gets it right, especially after they have seen your disappointed face. Happiness also conveys a contentment that gives those around you security for themselves and the team. There are times to push your team, and there are times to let them feel and see that you are pleased.

7. Always Pack a Sincere Face

Sincerity speaks of integrity and honesty. If the eyes are the windows to the soul, the face is the movie screen of one's intent. When you have to break bad news, you can be cold and distant to sterilize the delivery, but the person would feel much better if you delivered it with a glimpse of the pain that you truly feel. Sincerity must be expressed in the loving tact of serious honesty. Leadership at its core requires a trust that is evidenced in a sincere spirit. The way you share with others will reveal the very fabric of your integrity. Absolute honesty can be brutal. Sincerity will change the cold, hard facts into the truth with a loving tone. James Russell Lowell asserts, "Sincerity is impossible, unless it pervades the whole being."

> To be genuinely sincere requires you to intertwine your expressions with your ideas.

To be genuinely sincere requires you to intertwine your appearance with your ideas.

8. Always Pack an Optimistic Face

Optimism is a conscious choice. When someone looks to you for solutions, do they see your face validating the glass as half full or half empty? Colin Powell believes that "optimism is a force multiplier." A positive message is much stronger than one delivered with ambivalence. Optimism gives your ideas staying power.

If people were *Winnie the Pooh* characters, who do you like to be around, Tiggers or Eeyores? Tigger bounces everywhere and enjoys life even with obstacles. Even on great days, Eeyore expects it to get bad soon. No one likes a person who drains you of energy and joy. People like that can suck the very wind out of your sails, because they lack any optimism.

Pat Williams relates this great testimony to an optimistic face.

When Baseball Hall of Famer Tommy Lasorda retired after twenty years as manager of the Dodgers, I called him up and asked, "Tommy, what was the most important thing you did every day as a manager?" I thought he would talk to me about the strategic side of the game—the lineup card, getting the right match-ups, and so forth. But no, he said, "The most important thing I did was walk into the clubhouse the right way." "What do you mean?" I asked. "It's real simple," he replied. "It didn't matter whether we had won eight in a row or lost eight in a row. Whether things were great at home or not so great, I had to walk into the clubhouse the right way. The minute I came in, my players had to see an upbeat, positive manager. I had to walk straight, have a smile on my face, and an optimistic gleam in my eye. If my players had seen my chin at my belt buckle, the gloom would have spread like wildfire. It would have destroyed the ball club. You have to be optimistic all the time. That's a manager's most important job."[5]

The Right Place: Matching the Face with the Place

You have met people who always look angry, only to find them later to be pleasant. We know a leader who struggles with showing the appropriate face. He always seems to project a face that says, "We're teetering on the brink of failure." No one wants to get on the *Titanic* when the alarm is being sounded. To challenge someone with an expression of momentary struggle is acceptable, but to always be in this mode is unattractive. The discerning leader understands the choice of the face must be determined by the place.

> The faces you need to efficiently communicate to those around you must be intentionally collected, mentally packed, and frequently utilized.

The faces you need to efficiently communicate to those around you must be intentionally collected, mentally packed, and frequently utilized. What face are you wearing? In selecting the correct face, you must ask the following questions: *What feelings are people around me dealing with? What needs to be communicated? What is the most important thing I want them to see? What do I need to project in order to help them? How would I want them to look if our roles were reversed?* In answering these questions, you will meet needs rather than desires.

There are times that you, as the leader, must show an emotion that is completely different from your followers. You must, at times, project confidence when everyone feels failure, vision when others see a brick wall, and trust when trust has yet to be earned. But we also need to show disappointment when the margin of success is less than the team's capability.

The minute you walk into a room, someone is watching your face for a sign. They begin taking cues from you that will set the tone for the meeting, day, party, or event. Often we are unaware what we are speaking visually before we have even opened our mouth.

Like you, Ron makes these choices daily. Here is one such occasion:

Once in an airport, I failed to show the right face, and an employee let me know about it some time later. We were in production of a new line of curriculum and every member of the team was vital if we were to stay on schedule. Every person was stretched thin. I was traveling with our training team as we landed in Oklahoma City getting ready to speak at a major conference. One of our editors called back to the office as we were headed to the luggage carousel. When she hung up, she looked at me and said that a key member of our editorial staff had just resigned. Even though I knew her leaving was for family reasons, she was still a loss to the organization. In those fleeting seconds of searching for what to say, my mind raced through the implications of this resignation. So I reached into the compartment of faces and chose a cold, expressionless face and said, "Let's go get our luggage."

That editor later told me that she saw me put on the strong leader's face and ignore any emotion that she or I was feeling. She said that she wished I had put on an empathetic face, one that expressed the disappointment and anxiety that she, too, was feeling at the loss of a team member. She was right; I did not put on the right face in the right place that day.

There are times when you do not know which face to put on for the situation. You have to terminate a person—what is the correct face? If it is corporate downsizing, then an apologetic face may be in order. If it is employee negligence, then disappointment is probably best. If the position has outgrown an employee's abilities, then you had better have shown several faces at several points along the way so he realizes the bar is higher than he is capable of jumping. You must be conscious of the face you wear. Do you mask your emotions by not using facial expressions? Do you exaggerate facial expressions to belie your real feelings? Do you struggle with adequately expressing yourself? If you sense contradictions between your verbal and nonverbal messages, then there is room for improvement. If you find yourself constantly having your communication derailed, it may be because the face you are wearing is simply the wrong one.

> It's your first expression that makes the first impression.

Your face is a powerful instrument. Failing to wear the correct face is ultimately wearing the face of failure. Put these principles into practice, and you will be sending out a powerful message. Remember, it's your first expression that makes the first impression.

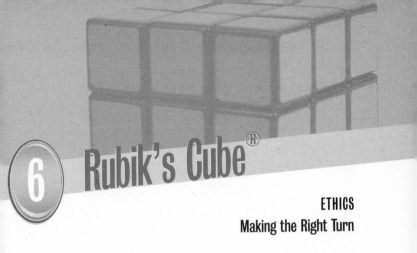

ETHICS
Making the Right Turn

If you are a child of the '80s, you probably remember parachute pants and Member's Only jackets. Big hair and skinny ties. Ronald Reagan and Madonna. Cabbage Patch Kids and Trivial Pursuit. However, no other icon epitomizes the 1980s like the Rubik's Cube® puzzle. It is colorful and complex—trendy yet timeless.

The Rubik's Cube® puzzle was invented in 1974 by a twenty-nine-year-old Hungarian architecture teacher named Ernö Rubik. In the Soviet Union, the marketing possibilities for the toy were limited, to say the least. But the puzzle finally broke through the Iron Curtain and was released worldwide six years later, selling over 100 million units by 1982. Ironically, this made Professor Rubik the first self-made millionaire from the Communist block. Some historians have even credited the capitalistic success of his invention as being the beginning of the end of the USSR. Over the last twenty-five years, people have purchased more than 250 million Rubik's Cube® puzzles, making it one of the best-selling toys in history.

Meanwhile, the fascination with Professor Rubik's puzzle continues to grow. This is one of the rare toys that has developed a cult following all its own. Disciples of the cube have met annually since 1982 to test their skill and time themselves as they search for the solution. The first recognized world record to completely solve the cube was 19 seconds. In 2006, the record shrunk to an astounding 10.48 seconds by Toby Mao at the U.S. Championships. A few other interesting world records to note are: one-handed—20.09 seconds; blind-folded—23.06 seconds; using feet only—1 minute 18 seconds; and number of cubes solved in a twenty-four-hour period—3,390.

These amazing records only underline the fact that while solving the Rubik's Cube® puzzle may look impossible, it is not. The solution to the chaos of the cube can be found one of two ways: by the book or by cheating. If "by the book" seems too difficult for you, Ron has his own method he wants to share:

> I can take a jumbled Rubik's Cube® puzzle and within two minutes have every color on their respective sides. My best time is about ninety seconds. There is just one catch—you have to close your eyes for that period of time. My ability to unscramble the cube comes by taking it apart, turning it

into twenty smaller cubes and one skeletal structure. Then I reassemble the cube and reveal the finished product. No one is ever impressed, because they are suspect of my methods, and rightly so.

Some people remove and reapply the colored square stickers, and others disassemble and reassemble the cube. To solve the cube correctly, it takes work and ethics, the kind that allow people to watch how you work with integrity. Whether people are watching or not, do not allow your ethics to be disassembled.

Many people look forward to the NCAA basketball tournament—better known as March Madness—when sixty-four of the best basketball teams in the country compete for the national title. This garners fans from all over the nation following their favorite team. In March 2006, a new phenomenon left employers across the country shaking their heads in frustration. You see, for the first time, CBS offered live coverage of the tournament online. According to Thomas Heath of the *Washington Post* in an article titled "Companies Fear Spread of March Madness," the NCAA tournament cost American businesses more than $3.8 billion in productivity.[1] In 2007, a new feature was added to the site, a "Boss Button." This button quickly brought up a fake spreadsheet to hide the fact that a person was watching the game instead of working. You may not be a sports fan, but what do *you* do that costs your company?

The qualities of the Rubik's Cube® puzzle that make it so intriguing are the same qualities that make it such a good example of ethics. It can be frustrating. It can seem impossible. You may be tempted to lay it aside. But as you see from the cube time records on page ninety-two, it can be done. The cube's color, depth, and dimensions represent the complexity of your ethics. As you solve the problems of life, this toy teaches the importance of making the right turns.

Cubism #1: Ethical Parallels in the Solution of the Cube

1. There Is an Acceptable Standard of Right

Just as the cube is not solved until each of the six sides has a solid color on it, there is an accepted standard of what is right in the business world. There are rules and expectations that form the standards of right. When searching for business books on ethics, you find few titles and very few pages among the best sellers on this subject. Rules and expectations don't end with Little League.

One cannot ignore the obvious absolute moral right. Regardless of your background or spiritual heritage, every person possesses an inherent sense of right and wrong. For example, no one would think it's acceptable for a boss to physically beat his employees. However, you might easily overlook someone reading a magazine at his workstation on company time. Obvious areas of right and wrong are easy to see in others and seem more obscure in our own lives. However, obscurity does not change the ethical principles.

When you do things correctly, it creates order. When you do them wrong, it creates chaos. Policies change, but principles of right never do. The leader is the solution to the mixed-up cube bringing order to the organization. When leaders enter the equation, they should bring a sense of right through their example for others to follow. No matter how mixed up the cube may become, the ultimate goal is to realign the colors to match on all six sides, and you as the leader must be the ethical catalyst.

People often believe you lose creativity and individuality when you have order and compliance. If this occurs, then you have confused ethics with ego and you are trying to make everyone like you rather than giving them guiding values. Order and compliance in ethical matters allow the whole group to be stronger in all areas, including creativity and distinctiveness. Ethics prevent one person from corrupting the office environment with her lack of scruples.

Behavior that is ethically, morally, and legally right should be the goal. The rules you live by and those you ignore will establish your character. You may find yourself at a loss for words, but you should never find

> The rules you live by and those you ignore will establish your character. You may find yourself at a loss for words, but you should never find yourself at a loss of values.

yourself at a loss of values. You know people who appear to do the right things on the surface while secretly crossing ethical boundaries. Secret boundary breakers are a lot like *The Queen Mary*, which served for four decades as a passenger liner and also saw service in World War II. Later she was to be converted into a museum and a hotel and permanently docked in Long Beach. But when they removed her three immense smoke stacks for repainting, the steel crumbled into millions of pieces. The thick steel of the walls had rusted away, leaving only the many coats of paint to maintain the structure. They looked great on the outside but had no substance on the inside, just like some leaders in corporate America.

2. There Are No Shortcuts in Ethics

One of the earliest ads by the Ideal Toy Company for the Rubik's Cube® puzzle boasted the cube had "43 Quintillion" possible moves but only "one" solution. The actual number of permutations is 43,252,003,274,489,856,000.[2] In spite of that number, every cube can be solved in twenty-seven moves or less. The key is knowing the right moves to make, because there are no shortcuts. There is only a right or a wrong move.

Unethical leaders try to see how much they can get away with or how far they can bend the rules. Companies like Enron and Adelphia would epitomize this mind-set because they took shortcuts that led to tragic results. Jon M. Huntsman, author of *Winners Never Cheat*, believes that "real winners never sneak to finish lines by clandestine or compromised routes. They do it the old-fashioned way—with talent, hard work, and honesty."[3] Go back a bit and you will recall one of the toughest decisions on ethics faced by a corporate giant: the financially wrenching decision to voluntarily recall thirty-one million bottles of Tylenol because someone tampered with eight bottles—injecting the capsules with cyanide and causing the deaths of several people. Can you imagine what it cost Johnson & Johnson to pull every bottle on the store shelves and in homes? That very costly decision serves as an example of integrity and ethics, and it resulted in Johnson & Johnson not closing its doors in 1982. They became a company you equate with trust, while Enron is tantamount to scandal.

3. Every Move Affects the Whole Cube

Most competitive cube solvers follow a set of algorithms and sequential moves. With each turn they know that the whole cube changes. The algorithms account for this and provide the formula to move every square toward perfection.

No one would think they could move one side of the cube without disturbing the other. Likewise, your organization is not lifeless. It is not a building. It is not a logo. Your organization is people. Your choices and decisions do not exist in a vacuum. They affect you, your employees, and the people your organization serves. Sometimes your choices are like ripples in a pond, easily traced back to the original source. Other times they are unseen, but like the wind they can still have a powerful effect.

Some damaging effects of wrong turns hit every employee at all levels. This occurs when you do not keep your word. Overpromising without delivering creates disappointment and a lack of confidence. Another wrong turn frequently overlooked by executives is nepotism. This occurs when a leader shows favoritism in the hiring or treatment of family members or close friends. Though you may conduct yourself with the purest of motives, this kind of partiality always creates odd office relationships. Even when family members or close friends are qualified and treated fairly by leadership, their peers usually sense an uneven playing field. Watch also for actions resulting in personal gains rather than organizational gains. Anytime you are the only beneficiary, you must stop to question your motives and your use of resources.

Cubism #2: Ethical Erosion in a Mixed-Up Cube

One glance at the headlines and you can sense our culture is in a moral meltdown. Business has Enron, baseball has steroids, the Catholic church has sexual abuse, and government has corruption. But it is not just the big companies and their leadership. It's regular people too—they just don't have CNN watching their every move.

For his recent best-selling book *The Cheating Culture*, David

Callahan interviewed people across America to determine the ethical status of our culture. He concluded that "cheating is everywhere." He writes that people are "breaking the rules to get ahead academically, professionally or financially. Some of this cheating involves violating the law; some does not. Either way, most of it is by people who, on the whole, view themselves as upstanding members of society."[4] Unfortunately, a philosophy today suggests, "If you ain't cheating, you ain't trying."

Leaders don't just wake up one day and say, "I think I'll be unethical today." Rather, there is a sequence of choices that slowly erodes a person's moral foundation. This happens in three eroding stages.

1. Mixed-Up Leaders Compromise Ethical Standards

People who have huge ethical failures can usually trace the beginnings back by small incremental degrees. They chose "small" wrongs because of convenience. At the time it seemed easier to lie than to face the consequences of the truth. Every white-collar crime begins with a compromise at trivial levels. This complacency gives way to numbness to the wrong values. And the wrong choices slowly become easier and more detrimental.

Like compromise, erosion is subtle and unnoticed. The National Oceanic and Atmospheric Administration estimates that in the next sixty years erosion will claim one out of every four houses that are within five hundred feet of the shoreline.

This major loss, believe it or not, begins with a single grain of sand. That is the nature of erosion—it claims pieces of dirt, then rocks, then yards, and eventually foundations, with the early progressions virtually undetected.[5] The incremental erosion of ethics will cause you to slowly acclimate to poor choices and a loss of integrity.

2. Mixed-Up Leaders Rationalize Unethical Decisions

The slow compromise of ethical standards is more easily accepted when you rationalize your actions. Most leaders climbed to where they are due to their ability to influence and communicate with others. Their ability to influence starts with their analytical mind and persuasive skills. Rationalization is an attempt to justify wrong choices. Leaders are not exempt from their own arguments of self-convincing persuasion, and that can result in conduct that is unprofessional or ethically off the chart.

This step begins with the lies you tell yourself. You do not call it a lie. Rather, you refer to it as a reason. That is how rationalizing is born in the minds of good leaders who start down the wrong road. When you start rationalizing, recognize it for what it is—an excuse. You will find yourself demonstrating rationalization when you tell yourself, "It's owed to me," "Don't they know all that I do for them?" "I deserve this," or "I will make this right later." You would not accept these rationalizations from your kids or your employees—so why would you accept excuses from yourself?

3. Mixed-Up Leaders Compartmentalize Unethical Behavior

At this stage unethical leaders will section off portions of their lives. It begins with a simple acceptance of a compromised standard. This is closely followed by rationalization to sooth their conscious. Then, to make the behavior even more palatable, they compartmentalize the unethical conduct.

Compartmentalization occurs when you take matters that are related to each other and put them in a separate mental section. It is here that unscrupulous behavior is accepted as normal business practice. You think as long as your actions are contained and separate from the rest of your life that they are manageable. At this point, allowing imperfections becomes the status quo.

A leader in this stage will find no problem with going to church on Sunday, proclaiming he loves his fellow man and the world around him—then on Monday allowing his company to release toxic waste into a neighborhood stream.

The primary motive for compartmentalization is comfort. You try to separate two dissonant portions of your life because it is too painful to have them revealed to each other. Lying to yourself is only the beginning; this list continues with your spouse, partner, coworkers, or board of directors. You may find comfort in this deception, but not integrity.

If you think you are immune, remember that compartmentalization is what sank the *Titanic*. The ship was designed using compartmentalized bulkheads, which supposedly made it unsinkable. The problem occurred when one flooded compartment spilled over into the next, and so on, until the ship was doomed. There are some things you just cannot perpetually contain, and unethical behavior is one of them.

Ethical Distinctives in a Multicolored Cube

Many people can contribute to chaos, but usually only a few can put it back in order. This is why ethical leadership is essential for long-term success. Ethics begins with leadership and should be expected by leadership. It's time leaders improve the character of their business rather than letting the business ruin their character.

> It's time leaders improve the character of their business rather than letting the business ruin their character.

The leaders who stand the test of time are those with solid ethical foundations. If you're going to model ethical behavior, the following four principles should become as natural to you as driving a car or breathing. They are like an internal ethical compass pointing the way to right.

1. Ethical Leaders Accept Responsibility

Have the courage to accept the consequences of your actions, and don't blame others to avoid looking bad. Your employees need to hear you take responsibility for a failed idea instead of shifting the blame. They already know you are not perfect; they just want to hear you acknowledge it. People need you to be the kind of leader who shows them the right action to take.

There is a great poem by Will Allen Dromgoole describing a man who did not need to prove anything because of the life he had lived, but went the extra mile anyway—listen to his reason why.

The Bridge Builder

An old man, going a lone highway,
Came at the evening, cold and gray,
To chasm, vast and deep and wide,
Through which was flowing a sullen tide.
The old man crossed in the twilight dim;
The sullen stream had no fears for him;
But he turned when safe on the other side
And built a bridge to span the tide.

"Old man," said a fellow pilgrim near,
"You are wasting strength with building here;
Your journey will end with the ending day;
You never again must pass this way;
You have crossed the chasm, deep and wide—
Why build you the bridge at the eventide?"
The builder lifted his old gray head:

"Good friend, in the path I have come," he said,
"There followeth after me today
A youth whose feet must pass this way.
This chasm that has been naught to me
To that fair-haired youth may a pit-fall be,
He, too, must cross in the twilight dim;
Good friend, I am building the bridge for him."[6]

Seize every opportunity to make sound moral judgments. Be the first to head down the path of integrity, and others will follow. This path is often the least taken because it may jeopardize the bottom line or cast shadows of weakness, but you'll find that integrity attracts more business and relationships for the long term than the alternative.

You can be the ethical catalyst for your organization by letting those around you know where you stand. Ambivalent integrity should not be one of your noticeable character traits. Right choices begin with you. If you think this point does not apply to you, remember the words of the comedian Steven Wright: "A clear conscience is usually the sign of a bad memory."

2. Ethical Leaders Desire Accountability

A leader with nothing to hide will welcome accountability. How important is accountability? Think about World-Com, Tyco, Adelphia, and Enron. In each of these cases a small group of people enriched themselves at the expense of shareholders and employees—all because of a lack of proper accountability.

There is not a leader in our country who is not accountable to someone. The president is accountable to the people, CEOs to their boards, board members to their shareholders, stockbrokers to their investors, and you, too, answer to someone. Most leaders would acknowledge a unique degree of accountability to their administrative assistant because of how much they know about their habits, time, personality, and temperament. Most assistants could easily tell how their boss's integrity ranks on a scale of 1 to 10. Your employees will always see more than you realize, and while they may still follow, it will be without the same zeal and trust if your actions reflect a lack of integrity.

3. Ethical Leaders Develop Integrity

Integrity doesn't have an on or off switch. Integrity isn't automatic—if it were, we would all be perfect. It must be intentionally established and carefully protected at every luring threshold. The question that then arises is, how is integrity maintained? The word *integrity* comes from the mathematics word *integer*, which means to be "whole and unified" or to be "complete and open." It means to be "undivided without duplicity or pretense," to be "consistent." What is on the inside is shown on the outside. Without this there can be no trust.

Trust is like sanding a board. To do it properly you must run the sandpaper with the grain to smooth the wood. One swipe of the sandpaper against the grain makes it rough, and then it takes about twenty passes with the grain to make it smooth again. When you lose trust by going against the grain of integrity, you must spend even more time with the grain in order to earn it back.

Integrity must be intentionally developed and maintained. "There is no such thing as a minor lapse of integrity"—that's how business management expert Tom Peters puts it in his book *Thriving on Chaos: Handbook for a Management Revolution.*

You earn the trust of people around you daily by doing the obvious. Start by keeping your word. If you do not keep your word, then you are giving away relationships. The decision to do what is right is ultimately yours. No employer or relationship should ever cause a lapse in your integrity.

Do not overpromise or under-deliver. No one likes hype or misleading packaging only to be disappointed by the product they receive. Remember that last product you felt you paid way too much for that did not live up to the sales pitch? You felt cheated and robbed. If you are under-delivering to your team, they feel just as cheated and probably will not stay long enough for you to do that to them more than a couple of times.

The distance between your belief and your action is equivalent to your

> The distance between your belief and your action is equivalent to your integrity.

integrity. Listen to one company's code of ethics: "We work with customers and prospects openly, honestly and sincerely. When we say we will do something, we will do it; when we say we cannot or will not do something, then we won't do it." This sounds good until you measure the distance between these words and the actions of the leaders who wrote them. Ironically, this quote is from Enron's Code of Ethics.[7]

In *Lincoln on Leadership*, Donald T. Philips writes, "The architecture of leadership, all theories and guidelines, falls apart without honesty and integrity. It's the keystone that holds an organization together."[8]

4. Ethical Leaders Make the Right Moves

Sometimes the best intentions in the world fall short. Gandhi wrote about seven social sins that began with good intentions:

1. Politics without principles

2. Wealth without work

3. Pleasure without conscience

4. Knowledge without character

5. Commerce without morality

6. Science without humanity

7. Worship without sacrifice[9]

You will notice that each of these began with a virtuous goal but at the expense of something vital to that goal. Judge your integrity not by your intentions but rather your actions. Check for the ingredients missing in your life. Ask yourself the following questions:

- Is this the right move morally?
- Is this the right move legally?
- Is this the right move ethically?
- Is this move right for everyone involved?

Remember the principle of the cube: every turn affects the whole cube. So make turns in business that create an ethical atmosphere through which the whole team becomes the recipient. Always turn toward truth, fairness, justice, care, patience, forgiveness, and helpfulness. Correctly blending these creates a high standard, which results in people believing that you are there to help them succeed.

The turns you and your employees make not only affect everyone in the organization but also reflect upon the reputation of the organization. Notice how Theodore Roosevelt handled the wrong turn of one of his employees. During his time as a rancher, Teddy Roosevelt and one of his cowpunchers lassoed a maverick steer, lit a fire, and prepared their branding irons. That part of the range they were on was claimed by

Gregor Lang, one of Roosevelt's neighbors. According to the cattleman's rule, the steer therefore belonged to Lang. As his cowboy began to apply the Roosevelt brand, Roosevelt said, "Wait, you should use Lang's brand." "That's all right, boss," said the cowboy. "Drop that iron," Roosevelt demanded, "and get back to the ranch and get out. I don't need you anymore. A man who will steal for me will steal from me."[10]

Does your organization have a mixed-up standard of right? A confused set of ethics? Are you prepared to lead it in making the right turns—creating order and integrity in all you do? Like the Rubik's Cube® puzzle, you have many possible moves each day, but only one right turn.

Rocking Horse

EFFICIENCY
All Show and No Go

The 1850s were a turbulent period in American history. The nation faced controversy over slavery, the aftereffects of the Mexican-American War, and the pressure to admit new states and territories into the Union. As if those problems weren't enough, President Zachary Taylor unexpectedly died of acute gastroenteritis. On July 9 of that year, Millard Fillmore was sworn in as the thirteenth president of the United States. President Fillmore, a Northerner, was very different from his predecessor, a Southerner, and the two had disagreed on many national policies. Fillmore's Whig party supporters sensed the political shift and assumed that all their problems were solved now that a new man was in office. President Fillmore understood their feelings, but he realized a greater truth when he stated, "It is not strange . . . to mistake change for progress."

People still make that mistake today when they try to substitute anything for genuine progress. They feel that motion and efficiency are synonymous. As long as they are doing something, they assume they're productive.

The rocking horse perfectly illustrates the faulty belief that actions equal progress. You can look and feel good while riding a rocking horse and yet get nowhere. Sadly, many leaders ride rocking horses every day, and in their minds they think they are making progress.

While all of the other toys in this book are lessons in the positive, the rocking horse is a lesson in the negative. It is a perfect example of how *not* to be efficient. When you were growing up, your mom or dad told you to not act like certain people, and they shared reasons why. We will do the same with the rocking horse and share with you why you don't want to be inefficient like him: all show and no go.

Michael has a humorous personal story that will help you never forget this truth:

> My first job as a minister was in a rural area in the panhandle of Florida. At Christmas, I was given a bonus that included five live chickens. With no previous poultry-related experience, I put them in the coop behind the church and was in the egg business overnight. A few months passed, and I had way too many chickens, so I decided to be a real farmer and fry one up. My wife wanted nothing to do with this, stating that she didn't want to eat any animal she had known personally, so she went to town. After she left, I walked into the chicken

coop, caught the slowest bird, and "wrung its neck" just as I had seen my grandmother do. Right before he died, this rooster (with a broken neck) went absolutely berserk. He jumped up, flew around wildly, and bounced off all four walls of that little cage. The other chickens just froze and watched him go. My point is this: the most active chicken in the pen at that moment was the one closest to death. Don't judge your efficiency solely by your activity.

The truth is that activity does not necessarily equate to progress. Movement does not automatically mean growth. Hard work does not guarantee success. Business leaders will tell you to work smarter, not harder, but how many explain what working smarter looks like? So, if you are in the saddle of the rocking horse, hang on, because you are in for a ride as we peel back one layer at a time the causes of inefficiency.

○   ○   ○

Active imaginations have fueled some great rocking-horse rides. They have been discovered in the pyramids of the pharaohs and excavated from the ruins of the Roman Empire. And like the historical rocking horse, your job can entertain, excite, enthuse, and exhaust you without ever moving you forward. How many times have you reached the end of the day only to look back and sigh that you have not accomplished anything? The lesson here is that efficiency is ultimately graded on progress, not motion. Type-A drivers are the worst in believing that movement equals progress. Have you ever seen one who goes around the block to avoid a red light just so he can keep moving?

George Bernard Shaw was right when he said, "There are only two qualities in the world: efficiency and inefficiency; and only two sorts of people: the efficient and the inefficient."

Widespread inefficiency has slowly compromised what is acceptable in the workplace. This has caused many leaders to lower their expectations of progress. The only thing worse than an inefficient person is a group of inefficient people. Watch as companies replace one person with two without changing their job responsibilities. Inefficiency often abounds when you avoid the needed analysis of the hiring process.

> The only thing worse than an inefficient person is a group of inefficient people.

Efficiency is being able to achieve a desired result without wasted time, energy, or resources. It is not concerned so much with the *act* of work as it is with the *results* of work. Do not jump to the conclusion that the outcome determines the measure of efficiency. Shortcuts and efficiency are not synonymous. Likewise, some streamlining may actually reduce the quality that defines your organization or product. A great example of this is Nordstrom's checkout procedure. When you purchase an item, the employee bags it, and instead of simply handing it over the counter to you, he or she carries the bag around the counter to you, providing not just a sale but a personal touch unlike any other. This proves that what may seem inefficient to some defines quality to others.

The first step to being efficient is defining it in your context. The definition of efficiency for your organization will point to the areas that need attention and warrant greater time investments. What consumes your time, energy, and resources? Analyze your return on these three, and you will understand how efficient you really are.

To better understand where you are right now, see if you are riding one of the following four inefficient horses.

Four Types of Inefficient "Rocking Horses"

The Dead Horse

Dead horses can describe people, departments, and programs—anything that has outgrown its usefulness or is not contributing to the overall forward momentum. Organizations often perpetuate ineffective programs without questioning if there's a better way to reach greater results. Perpetual programs often exist because they met a need twenty years ago.

The March of Dimes was established to find a cure for polio, but when the cure came, they had to ask if they were still needed. They took their skills and applied them to other diseases, becoming effective in many areas, especially relating to the wellness of newborns. We could all benefit from asking if we need to retool our programs to better meet today's needs.

We should examine positions within our organization. No matter how hard the people in those positions work, their function must be relevant to the company's purpose. When a person's job is obsolete, he or she may be defined as a dead horse. Leaders who protect dead horses jeopardize the future of the organization, and such business decisions may cost many more jobs than those they are protecting.

These individuals within the organization who are dead horses did not die overnight. They may have euthanized themselves over time by refusing to keep current with the skills of their trade or career. They work themselves out of a job and then blame others when they are let go.

Sometimes the climate changes and people simply don't need the service offered. In the '80s, you saw people succeeding in businesses that sold pagers or beepers, but that quickly became a dead-horse service with the increased popularity of cell phones. Organizations today are guilty of having people or programs that are dead horses.

The tribal wisdom of the Dakota Indians, passed on from one generation to the next, says that when you discover you are riding a dead horse, the best strategy is to dismount. However, in modern business, because of the heavy investment factors to be taken into consideration, we often try other strategies, including the following:

1. Buying a stronger whip

2. Changing riders

3. Threatening the horse with termination

4. Appointing a committee to study the horse

5. Arranging to visit other sites to see how they ride dead horses

6. Lowering the standards so that dead horses can be included

7. Appointing an intervention team to reanimate the dead horse

8. Creating a training session to increase the rider's load share

9. Reclassifying the dead horse as living-impaired

10. Changing the form so that it reads, "This horse is not dead."

11. Hiring outside contractors to ride the dead horse

12. Harnessing several dead horses together for increased speed

13. Donating the dead horse to a recognized charity, thereby deducting its full original cost

14. Providing additional funding to increase the horse's performance

15. Conducting a time management study to see if the lighter riders would improve productivity

16. Purchasing an after-market product to make dead horses run faster

17. Declaring that a dead horse has lower overhead and therefore performs better

18. Forming a quality focus group to find profitable uses for dead horses

19. Rewriting the expected performance requirements for horses

20. Promoting the dead horse to a supervisory position[1]

The Hobby Horse

You have seen people preoccupied with their own interests. They lack dedication to the company purpose. Examine your team's daily actions to determine if they fit with their job descriptions. Accountants use the term *water-cooler time* to describe unproductive periods that are on the clock. An honest executive will recognize that a certain amount of social swapping of stories helps morale. However, it would be interesting to determine how much water-cooler time has expanded since technological advancements such as personal cell phones, the Internet, blogging, text messaging and instant messaging. Todd

Duncan writes in *Time Traps*, "Technology led us to the wonders of timesaving devices. But these days, the timesaving devices we laud as efficient may be stealing the very thing they were designed to save."[2] You are riding the rocking horse when you are spending too much time in these areas. Imagine a virtual stopwatch with two displays above your head. The clock on the left runs when you are working, and the one on the right runs when you are on your rocking horse. It may surprise you how often you take your company for a ride.

> It may surprise you how often you take your company for a ride.

Everyone has tasks they prefer not to do. You sometimes go out of your way to avoid these tasks and feel justified when you do not have time to do them. Instead you fill your day with tasks that fail to meet the company's objectives. According to the Conference Board, the world's preeminent business membership and research organization, two out of three employees do not feel motivated to support their employer's business objectives.[3] You must conquer certain tasks, even when you do not enjoy them, the same way you had to pass certain subjects in school.

While you may be quick to observe this behavior in those around you, be careful to not fool yourself into thinking you are exempt. Pause for a moment at lunch and at the close of each business day and check your own virtual stopwatch.

The High Horse

This person is the prototypical bureaucrat. His personal agenda supersedes the company purpose. In fact, he believes the company exists to meet his needs, not that he was hired to meet the company's needs. While this attitude exists at every level, it is most unsuitable in leadership. Leaders without prudence display an extravagance that is inappropriate for the situation. "In June 1544, Philip the Prudent sailed to wed Mary Tudor in England, his father ordered him to go with 'minimum of display.' So he took only 9,000 nobles and servants, 1,000 horses and mules, three million ducats in gold, and a mere 125 ships."[4] Philip certainly rode a high horse, and those leaders today who ride one make others question their motivations.

High-horse riders typically have ulterior motives. You can picture that person whose every action is self-serving and motivated by his own agenda. The high-horse rider destroys morale and lacks trust from the team. If you can remove your selfish interests and work for the organization's goals, then you as the leader will be able to challenge your team to do the same while gaining long-term results. In *The Attention Deficit Workplace*, Mitch Thrower writes, "Naked, not veiled, agendas will turbo-boost your productivity and efficiency."[5]

The Wild Horse

This person is a rebel. She lacks direction regarding company purpose, choosing a renegade route instead. The wild horse is called wild because it is not broken or tamed. She despises the rider because the rider tries to steer her to a destination not of her own choosing. People who cannot take direction are wild horses who have little value within a team. Tame the horse or turn her out of your corral.

Rocking Horse Riders

Many people will remain on the rocking horse their whole career, riding year after year without accomplishment. Some people feel that as long as they are busy, they are making progress. Busyness makes them feel important, but Henry David Thoreau wrote, "It is not enough to be busy. The question is: What are we busy about?"

Sometimes people are stuck on the horse because they just don't understand what to be busy about. They did not start out riding a rocking horse, but they could not tell you when they swapped saddles from a real workhorse.

Inefficient people are rocking horse riders who lack the following five properties.

Rocking Horse Riders Lack Information

As a leader, you need to give your team the information they need to see the big picture or understand your direction. Don't cause them to waste hours hunting for ideas and answers that you can easily provide. The only thing worse than searching for something is not knowing the object of your search. Some leaders tell their employees what tasks to do without telling them the end result or goal. Employees who know the end result and are given a little latitude may prove more efficient through a different method than your own. When giving people a new goal or project, spot-check them for added efficiency about a third of the way into the work. This prevents frustration and wasted time if they head in the wrong direction, rather than discovering it upon completion.

Rocking Horse Riders Lack Ambition

People without ambition accept the status quo. There is an old business cliché that says employees work just hard enough to not get fired and employers pay the employees just enough so they won't quit. Ambition is the inner drive to achieve the self-satisfaction that you have accomplished something meaningful. Ambitious people are typically passionate people, translating into determination that will not quit.

Sadly, many people are satisfied with little or no progress at all. They get a paycheck and have established routines that make them comfortable. They just don't want to expend the energy required to be

> History books never record mediocrity, nor do we see statues built for people who were average.

effective because they have no ambition. History books never record
mediocrity, nor do we see statues
built for people who were average.
The Smithsonian has no exhibits
for achieving the status quo. People
want to follow leaders who can
stretch the possibilities and distance
themselves from run-of-the-mill

> People want to follow leaders who can stretch the possibilities and distance themselves from run-of-the-mill progress.

progress. Lou Vickery knows about progress. He has suc-
ceeded as a professional baseball player, a stockbroker, and an
author. He said, "Nothing average ever stood as a monument
to progress."[6]

Rocking Horse Riders Lack Meaningful Goals

People often have goals, just the wrong ones. They spend
much of their time working on the unimportant or chasing
tasks that are completely irrelevant. Do you set goals for the
future? When you have long-term goals, do you set daily or
weekly tasks to help you achieve them? You must have the correct intermediate tasks to accomplish your long-term goals.
Without goals and tasks, how do you measure your efficiency?
If you set goals and yet consistently do not reach them, then
you are riding a rocking horse. Pastor and author Ed Trenner
stressed the importance of goals when he said, "Life without
goals is like a race without a finish line."

Rocking Horse Riders Lack Direction

People who lack direction have no idea how to set goals because they do not know where they need to go. They operate even though they are unsure of their purpose. Working without direction is like a vacation without a destination. Direction tells you where you should go based upon your information, ambition, and goals.

> Working without direction is like a vacation without a destination.

Have you ever called a company only to get a recorded voice welcoming you to their organization, inviting you to press numbers to get information? If you detest pushing twenty-four buttons to get to the person you need, then you should also detest pointless meetings or tasks leaving you no closer to making progress. You may have heard the joke about the salesman driving around with his boss. After a long period of silence, the salesman said to his boss, "The bad news is we are lost; however, the good news is we are making great time!" Businesses are full of people doing the wrong things but making great time. Unfortunately, quality doesn't matter if you are doing the wrong job.

Rocking Horse Riders Lack Focus

These riders lack focus, which translates into not concentrating on the correct area of responsibility. When you lack focus, your clarity transforms into ambiguity. You don't know how to stay on task or follow through to completion. You can manage your time once you manage your distractions.

What distracts you? For some, answering e-mails all day determines their priorities. For others, it is opening their mail, and then three catalogues later they have wasted twenty minutes. Whether it is randomly surfing the Internet, listening to colleagues retelling the same stories, or running unplanned errands, there are limitless ways to substitute wasted actions for our to-do list.

> You can manage your time once you manage your distractions.

You can easily get into the downward spiral of regularly choosing the wrong priorities. You waste time on unimportant tasks. Sometimes you even waste time on flawed time-saving systems. Ultimately, you may be a rocking-horse cowboy in denial. It is time to break that habit and give that horse some legs.

Giving Your Horse Legs

The first priority is the ability to gauge efficiency. If you have no benchmark of measure, then how will you know if you are wasting time? Here are a few ways to get yourself out of the gate:

- Set long-term goals every year.

- Set intermediate goals every month or quarter.

- Set weekly goals to reach the intermediate ones.

- Set daily tasks to reach the weekly goals.

- Measure your results every day with reflection and checklists.

- Watch your bottom line.

Through this personal story, Ron shows how simple this principle is and how looking at the people around you helps you to recognize when you are being inefficient.

When I was six I went to the department store with my grandfather, and he would put a quarter in the horse out in front of the store for me to ride. I knew it was a good day if I could talk him into a two-quarter ride. I imagined being a marshal and riding hard and long. At the end of the ride, my grandfather would get up from the bench beside the horse ride and say, "You rode a long time not to get very far." I understand that lesson more today than ever before, and I try to get off before fooling myself into believing I am going somewhere.

Jacques Rousseau was a Swiss philosopher whose political ideas influenced the French Revolution. He used a great example from the Bible to illustrate how most inefficient people respond:

Remember the parable of talents [coins]—the story of the three servants who had received talents, five, two and one respectively? When their master returned they all gave account of their stewardship. The first two had doubled their capital. Each of them said so in sixteen words, and their work was pronounced, "Well done, good and faithful servant." The third servant had accomplished absolutely nothing, but his report took forty-three words, three times as long as each of the other two reports. Don't be like servant number three. Make good! Don't explain your failure! Do the thing you are expected to do! Then you won't have to explain why you didn't, couldn't, wouldn't, or shouldn't. Making good required no explanation. Failure required forty-three words.

Aim for efficiency. Don't make excuses—just get off that horse. Rocking horses are inefficient—all show and no go. Leaders cannot afford to be inefficient. The horse you ride determines your response to accountability.

One final word of warning: be careful of sharing your newfound knowledge of efficiency with certain people. Once, an efficiency expert concluded his lecture with a similar note of caution. "You don't want to try these techniques at home." "Why not?" asked somebody from the audience. "I watched my wife's routine at breakfast for years," the expert explained. "She made lots of trips between the refrigerator, stove, table, and cabinets, often carrying a single item at a time. One day I told her, 'Hon, why don't you try carrying several things at once?'" "Did it save time?" the guy in the audience asked.

"Actually, yes," replied the expert. "It used to take her twenty minutes to make breakfast. Now I do it in seven."

8 Little Green Army Men

It's one of the few times a five-year-old slows down. Just pour out a bag of little green army men and watch. Their minds give strategic consideration to each soldier and its meticulous placement. The time they spend setting up their army is enormous in comparison to the time it takes to play out the battle. Little green army men prove that success is in the setup.

Toy soldiers have been toy box regulars for centuries. Tiny military figures have been found in Egyptian tombs and Prussian palaces. They grew to their greatest popularity in the seventeenth century, at which time they were mass-produced for wargames as a pastime for the aristocracy of the day. Today, worldwide societies remain dedicated to the art of miniature war-gaming with toy soldiers.

Through the years these soldiers have been constructed from clay, wood, flour, paper, and sundry metals. In the late 1940s, with the development of plastics and the advent of the Second

World War, they took the form and the name they retain today—little green army men. Though they have changed colors and weapons, they remain a favorite of children around the world. They have even made the jump to digital by becoming the star of a series of video games by 3DO.

○　○　○

It is in the moments of setting up those miniature toys that children formulate strategic plans of strike and counterstrike. They learn that good plans take careful thought, contain multiple steps, and create endless scenarios. Those little soldiers teach you that careful preparation increases your odds for victory. Henry Ford taught this principle when he said, "Before everything else, getting ready is the secret of success."

For the leader, superior planning is more than keeping a to-do list and a calendar. It involves a calculated strategy and an intentional planning process. Whether in business or in your personal life, you have to dedicate yourself to planning to achieve positive results. "The will to win is not nearly as important as the will to prepare to win"—that's how Bobby Knight, the winningest coach in the history of men's college basketball, puts it. Wins seldom come without careful setup and commitment to that plan.

Planning consists of analysis, preparation, practice, and further analysis. The military utilizes checkpoints for a myriad of reasons, but at the heart of every checkpoint lies accountability.

Checkpoints measure the movement of people, inspect what they are carrying, determine how fast they are moving, and evaluate what types of people are involved. Let's examine five checkpoints that provide success in the setup or strategy phase. Remember, you must work through these in the order presented.

The Checkpoint of Involvement

When children pour out a bag of army men, they automatically get down on the floor with the troops. You just can't play with army men from a distance. The same is true in your setup phase. Your viewpoint must be the same one as the people with whom you are planning. By definition, strategic planning is grand in scale—focused on the big picture—and yet the place to start is on the ground. Gone are the days of unchecked power, lack of accountability, and the great gulf between management and labor. It is time to get to know those who work within the organization.

Herb Kelleher, the cofounder and former CEO of Southwest Airlines, understood the power of getting to know the people within his organization at every level. An article about Kelleher written by Allan Cohen, James Watkinson, and Jenny Boone recounts a time he traveled to congratulate a team for their outstanding performance and the impact it had on one of his employees:

During his visit Herb took the time to speak with everyone, and Grant [Grant Bowker, the station supervisor] remembers how Herb asked about his family and children. Grant appreciated the genuine consideration that Herb showed to everyone, but it was their second meeting 2 years later that stuck in his mind, when Herb arrived to celebrate the launch of a new plane and upon seeing Grant he remembered his name and asked how his children were doing—also by name.[1]

In the classic leadership book *In Search of Excellence*, Tom Peters calls this MBWA, or "Managing By Walking Around."[2] This practice allows you to really understand the people you lead. Two of the best by-products of MBWA are open communication and genuine trust that develops within your team. Five minutes of face-to-face personal contact will do more than a week's worth of e-mails. Instead of calling

> Five minutes of face-to-face personal contact will do more than a week's worth of e-mails.

people to your office, consider meeting them in theirs. It is less threatening, and yet your presence is felt around the office. It requires more time but connects you with the people who get the real work done.

Get to know your organization. Get down where the action is; talk with people at all levels. Ask questions and listen. A couple of questions to ask are "What project are you working on now?" and "What obstacles are you facing?" There is no substitute for firsthand knowledge of the people, the programs, and the problems the people face. You cannot effectively reach the next checkpoint until you know your team. Remember, strategy begins at ground zero.

The Checkpoint of Assessment

As children start to play with army men, they look them over to see what they have. They count how many and what kinds. There's the radioman, the flamethrower, the crawling guy, and every child's least favorite: the minesweeper. You can't know your organization's potential until you know the potential of your people. Even a five-year-old understands there is purpose in their differences.

> You can't know your organization's potential until you know the potential of your people.

It's amazing to watch children actually go through something very similar to the SWOT analysis with the little green army men even though they have never heard of this principle before. The SWOT analysis helps plan strategies and is credited to Albert Humphrey, who first used this method while leading a research project at Stanford University. SWOT is the analysis of an organization's strengths, weaknesses, opportunities, and threats. When applying this to your planning, you must recognize that strengths and weaknesses are typically internal descriptions, while opportunities and threats are typically external issues. SWOT sounds a lot like planning for battle, and kids at play figured this out ages before it was a staple in business schools.

You can see the wheels turning in the child's mind as he works through the setup of his little green army men. The strategy involves analysis and planning through various areas of counting. Just like the child, you count three different areas in this stage of planning.

1. Count the Troops

This is a quantity inventory. How many people do you have to tackle this project? Take into consideration the ratio of people needed proportionate to the project. This information is important because the group you lead sets the limits of some strategy. Bill George, the former CEO of Medtronics, states in his book *Authentic Leadership*, that "to build a top quality team around you, it is essential early in your tenure to assess whether you have the people in place who can enable the organization to reach its long-term goals."[3]

The questions to ask in this stage are: Who is available? Who is necessary? Who has potential? Who is in the wrong place? If the count of people is not proportionate to the task or project, then you can recruit more people or adjust the task to an intermediate level of accomplishment. Some people fail not because of dreadful planning but from underestimating the required number of people or their level of talent. Even a child knows you never tackle a whole mechanized company of armored vehicles with just a squad of riflemen.

2. Count the Types

This is a quality inventory. This maps your current capabilities. There's far more talent in your people than you are aware. Find it, challenge them, and they will step up with eagerness to work within their passions and strengths. Jeffrey Pfeffer and Gerald Salancik, authors of *The External Control of Organizations: A Resource Dependence Perspective* say, "The key to organizational survival is the ability to acquire and maintain resources." Do you really know what is at your disposal? If you are getting to know your people, you will find some hidden strengths and passions that could be a real asset to the organization.

To count your talent level, look beyond the surface of what you know. Marcus Buckingham, in *The One Thing*, recommends that leaders discover what is unique about each person in their organization and then capitalize on those uniquenesses.[4] Understanding the types of people and their capabilities prevents you from taking your best accounting person and asking him to work in the R&D area, or putting a salesperson in charge of asset management. Counting the types holds you accountable.

Properly utilizing your resources will result in the greatest advancement toward your goal. In the book *Good to Great*, Jim Collins compares planning to being a bus driver. He says to be successful you have to "get the right people on the bus first and

> Properly utilizing your resources will result in the greatest advancement toward your goal.

the wrong people off the bus" before you can decide which direction to drive.[5]

3. Count the Time

This is a chronological inventory. Time for planning must be a priority. Begin by counting the time allotted for a project. One invaluable time principle taught by the military is called backward planning. Backward planning simply teaches you to start at the end and work backward to where you are now, getting a glimpse of what success looks like at each step. If ten is the endpoint, what would nine look like and how do we get from step eight to nine? Repeat this all the way back to step one, making a list of all the tasks needed to achieve each step. This will cover equipment, time, and personnel needed for each step. Backward planning is most effective when the first portion of time allotted is given over to planning the reverse steps needed to achieve the goal. Usually kids set up the front lines of the little green army men first and then work back to the support troops.

The most common timing mistakes leaders make are not allowing enough time for planning, or running out of time halfway through the plan. Give steps four through nine due diligence. Many leaders are visionary enough to dream up lofty goals but become discouraged while working through the tedious intermediate steps. They dream of reaching ten but quit around step three. Just as a child asks, "Are we there yet?" you can be impatient in reaching your goals. Count your time as you would read a map. While it may take longer than anticipated, you can gauge how close you are to your destination.

Look for approaching windows of opportunity. You can use windows of extra time for launching new programs without upsetting the normal workflow. If you miss one window, grab another. If you miss two windows for a launch, then question the launch. You may have missed the most opportune time.

Block periods of time to evaluate your progress. Take time each week to decide what you need to accomplish the next week and the next month. Take larger blocks once a year to evaluate your annual progress in comparison to where you want to be in two or three years. If you are not planning backward, then you may be losing battles before they start. You should dedicate most of the time you've allowed for a task to preparation. Allow at least a four-to-one ratio of planning to execution. Don't rush it.

Printers have a favorite saying for those who want a print

job done overnight: "Your lack of prior planning does not constitute an emergency on my part." People around you do not want to be reacting to your lack of preparation.

The Checkpoint of Placement

After involvement and assessment comes the arranging. This third phase involves the positioning of people. At this point you place individuals according to the plan, and that requires strategic thinking. This placement sensitizes them to their significance in the setup. Colman Mockler, CEO of Gillette, asserted that "every minute devoted to putting the proper person in the proper slots is worth weeks of time later."[6] There are three facets of positioning the right people in the right place.

The "Who" of Positioning

The "who" of positioning people is based upon the talent needed. We have all made the mistake of making a bad hire. Bad hires are based upon the wrong selection criteria needed for a job. For example, a bad hire is banishing a person with excellent people skills to cubical city, without interaction with customers. Not only have we just placed a round peg in a square hole, but we have limited her potential and impaired her desire for longevity with the company. People can be trained to do something outside their talents, but relegating them to that role is strategic failure.

You may not be able to hire a whole new team, but moving the round pegs to round holes will give your team new life. You could have the personnel needed but not have them arranged based upon their abilities. In other words, you have the right people in the wrong places. The authors of *The Discipline of Getting Things Done* suggest that "leaders need to commit as much as 40 percent of their time and emotional energy, in one form or another, to selecting, appraising, and developing people."[7] Realistic job descriptions offer the beginning framework of the strategic plan. If you are disappointed in an employee, ask yourself if he knew the standard of work expected before you express that disappointment to him. He is not failing if he never had a standard by which to measure his work.

In *Now Discover Your Strengths*, Marcus Buckingham and Donald O. Clifton advise that great organizations "must watch for clues to each employee's natural talents and then position and develop each employee so that his or her talents are transformed into bona fide strengths."[8] The second-worst mistake a leader can make at this checkpoint is ignoring people's specialized abilities. The worst mistake that will keep an organization from reaching its potential is protecting a weak link in the team who refuses to step up and adapt even after being given several chances.

Don't make a move without assessing talent and personalities. While there are many personality tests available, we believe the "Leading from Your Strengths" personality assessment is the most enlightening and effective for employee placement and hires within an organization. This assessment comes from the *Team Building Discovery Kit* by Dr. John Trent and Rodney Cox.[9] You will find that using this training tool results in better performance, higher job satisfaction, and enhanced employee morale.

Even when you give your best effort, there will be times when people are not willing to move to their strengths. Make every attempt to help them both personally and publicly by coaching, training, or reassigning. Should you need to terminate them at that point, take comfort in knowing that you protected them according to their commitment level.

Just as organizations must be challenged to reach new goals, people also must be challenged. If not, sometimes they are content to continue to do what they have always done. Significant progress is never made by doing things the same old way. You will never see a company that over many years does not regularly update the way in which their people tackle their everyday tasks in order to stay in business. Organizations that refuse to change their methods to meet demands are likely the same stubborn organizations that are slowly going out of business.

> Organizations that refuse to change their methods to meet demands are likely the same stubborn organizations that are slowly going out of business.

The "Where" of Positioning

The "where" of positioning is determining the place people are needed. With your well-thought-out backward plan, the "where" should become obvious. Even the child knows that the little green army man holding the bazooka (or in modern-day terms, light anti-tank weapon) must be positioned where you expect tanks to be coming. Put him in a dense forest, and you have wasted firepower.

Leadership expert John Maxwell explains the potential of this step like this: "The right person in the right place equals progression, and the right people in the right places equals multiplication."[10] The truth is that being in the right place at the right time often compensates for having minimal talent. The best marketing message on a billboard beside a dirt road has less impact than an average message alongside the interstate.

People placement is about scenario logistics. Knowing the desired scenario allows you to place people according to how and where they best contribute to making this scenario happen. When you sufficiently practice the checkpoint of placement, it allows plans to move fluidly, precisely, and efficiently.

The "When" of Positioning

The "when" of positioning is determining the time people are needed. Knowing your people allows you the luxury of moving someone at the precise time needed for them to be successful. Sometimes you know the place a person is needed, but the timing may not be right for one reason or another. Here is how Ron executed this principle in the planning for a new division:

> I knew that a certain manager was extremely gifted in computer technology and would be overwhelmingly qualified to lead the new digital division. This manager was also one of the key architects on another project he helped design and launch. I was patient in moving this manager only after finding a replacement for his current position so as not to lose ground and to prepare for both managers' successes.

If results are necessary, timing truly is everything when people and events are involved. In business, you have seen people do the right thing at the wrong time, with adverse consequences.

The Checkpoint of Development

Once all the army men are counted and in the right place at the right time, the battle can commence. The turning point of the setup process is when preparation encounters modification, and you have to adapt your plan to fit the changing circumstances, sometimes before the action has even started. Solid planning always meets with adaptation. You must expect the plans to be in flux during development. Andy Stanley writes, "A leader who is not willing to revise his plan will rarely reach his destination."[11] The best strategy takes time to evolve and evolves over time. Jack Welch taught his employees that "change is never over."[12]

Once implementation begins, don't second-guess the little things unless they are vital to the overall success. The temptation is to rehash what you have already worked through early in the process. Many times those little items are the nervous "what ifs" that distract from where you should be focused. So how do you know if it's a little thing or not? There are three criteria that will distinguish the trivial from the important, influence your plan, and cause adjustments prior to implementation.

Practical Rehearsal

In the infantry, they recognize the value of "sand box" rehearsals, and troops use them regularly during training. A platoon sees on a small scale—called a "sand box"—a representation of the real-life operation. Using a terrain model, they see the who, what, when, and where of each action, which creates a familiarity when implemented. Practicing is usually relegated to the world of sports and war, but you will be surprised at the benefits of some informal rehearsal at your workplace. Going through the motions before the actual performance will give even the most timid person a needed boost of confidence. Walk your team through emergency action drills, team presentations, or product rollouts. The implementation should never be the first time you have gone through the motions of a task.

Proactive Policymaking

Intuitive leadership sets policies in place not as a nuisance but as a guide for people to know what is expected. Good policies encourage creativity and productivity with unnecessary restrictions. Policies should anticipate problems rather than react to them. Writing policies before they are needed saves hurt feelings. There's an old saying that you should implement a two-signature business check policy before two signatures are needed.

Planned Contingencies

Anticipate problems and build in contingencies. During your execution, it will be obvious that even though you spent months planning, you could not anticipate every obstacle. Planned adjustments, with trigger points, are easier because it allows everyone to be on the same page. Contingencies may allow for a change in methodology, timing, people involved, or even the tasks. Tell people, "If X occurs, we will do the following." When X occurs, it will be like a starter's pistol launching people into contingency mode without being told. Contingency planning reduces the stress of obstacles and problems by giving people options. Use contingencies for short-term plans, not long-term goals. Long-term goals

provide windows of collaborative adjustment where you rarely
need quick contingencies.

The Checkpoint of Refinement

The checkpoint of refinement is commonly referred to in the
military as an "after-action review." When you refine, you
improve something by the removal or addition of something
else. This adjustment will enhance your next plan, making it
stronger and more effective. If you believe you can improve
yourself (as advocated in chapter 3, "Play-Doh®"), then logi-
cally you will agree that processes and systems can likewise be
improved. Employees often get anxious when leaders address
improvement opportunities because they usually point out
shortcomings. In contrast, they will readily gravitate to a system that is part of their routine rather than the big stick of
administration. As significant as this checkpoint is, refinement regularly gets left out of planning.

Here are a few ways to make the refinement checkpoint
part of your business culture. With every event, from the
seemingly insignificant workday to a major product launch,
give people permission to critique the process. Encourage
them to make notes on the spot, adjust where needed, and
save the notes for the after-action review. Very soon after the
launch, event, testing, etc., sit down with those involved and
find out what went well and what could have gone better.

Make notes at this meeting so you can use it for the next event or rollout. Ken Blanchard says, "I believe providing feedback is the most cost-effective strategy for improving performance and instilling satisfaction."[13] When people understand the refinement process exists to help them and not to rebuke them, they will own their job quality daily.

○   ○   ○

As plain as little green army men are in form, the principles they teach are profound. They have no moving parts, no accessories or batteries—they are rather simple. Like the army men, the essence of efficient strategy is simplicity. Hit the checkpoints of involvement, assessment, placement, development, and refinement through backward planning and you will find yourself winning more battles than you lose. It is very easy for people to get lost in complex, time-consuming, or overly technical procedures. When a strategic plan gets too complicated, nobody bothers to follow it anyway. All you really need to be successful in strategic planning can be learned from those little plastic soldiers.

9 Lite-Brite®

Clark Byers's paintings numbered over nine hundred, and they were displayed in nineteen states. If you have traveled anywhere around the Southeast, you have probably seen one. Although he didn't know it at the time, Clark was at the center of perhaps the most understated—albeit successful—attempts to get across a message in history.

The year was 1932, and Garnet Carter's newly opened attraction in Chattanooga was feeling the effects of the Great Depression. To attract customers he hired a young sign painter to travel the countryside offering to paint farmers' barns for free in exchange for letting him paint one catchy little phrase on the roof. Three simple yet effective words: "See Rock City." So simple, yet so effective. For three decades Clark painted, leaving his distinct black-and-white mark on barns and birdhouses as far north as Michigan and as far west as Texas. You may never have been to Chattanooga to actually see Rock City, but if you ever read one of his signs, you wanted to.

The "See Rock City" campaign is recognized as one of the most creative examples of getting across a point that the world has seen in the last hundred years. Its simplicity conveyed a clear message that evoked a desire to accept the invitation; it employed an easily understood design; and it utilized a unique and readily available media. This campaign delivered a compelling message to the best audience: travelers who were driving toward Chattanooga.

The signs were so memorable that they have truly become part of the American cultural landscape—in fact, one of Clark's birdhouses even hangs in the Smithsonian. All that from an idea and a bucket of paint. Now that's a powerful message.

Today our culture has gone from "barn painting" to digital billboards, from paper letters to e-mails. In fact, most of the technological advances in the last thirty years grew from the need to communicate faster, more efficiently, and more effectively. You probably use e-mail, instant messaging, cell phones, texting, and video conferencing. But even with all these convenient methods of communication at your disposal, there is no guarantee that your message will be understood as it was intended. Electronic communication is one of the most misunderstood mediums because it lacks your emotional expression to aid in understanding. That's why those little smiley face expressions came into being :-) . In fact, e-mails and texting have a causal effect in that messages are abbreviated to such an extreme that the reader is often left confused. So how can you be sure to peg your point every time? Follow the example of the Lite-Brite® toy: illuminate to communicate.

From its beginning, the Lite-Brite® toy has always been about constructing and presenting a message. Inventor Marvin Glass introduced this art toy in 1967 as an electric alternative to painting. Hasbro loved the idea because it capitalized on a growing trend of "creative toys" without the mess of chalk or paints. Parents must have loved it too, since it became a national fad by Christmas of that year. This toy is still popular in various forms today. There is the classic one, the Lite-Brite® cube (with screens on four sides), the flat-screen version, and even an online version at www.hasbro.com/litebrite/swf/litebrite.cfm.

Here is an example of how entrenched our culture's experience with this toy is: On January 31, 2007, in Boston, Interference Incorporated, an advertising firm, launched a campaign for the *Aqua Teen Hunger Force* movie by putting up LED cartoon figures across the city. After the electronic devices were mistaken for bombs, the authorities and the media chose the only word that people would understand to adequately describe the devices. They called them an "upscale version of Hasbro's Lite-Brite®," and immediately everyone got the picture.[1]

You may remember your first Lite-Brite® toy—taking it out of the box, placing the black paper in front of the light bulb, grabbing those translucent multicolored pegs, and poking them into the holes, allowing the light to shine through. Do you remember the first picture you formed with those pegs? For many kids it was their name. Every child wants to see his or her name in colorful lights. After growing up, many people still want to see their name in lights, but successful leaders would rather see their message.

○   ○   ○

Some people think communication is easy. After all, they talk their whole lives. But even the most gifted communicators have trouble some days. Have you experienced this? For a leader, there is nothing worse than sitting face-to-face with someone and feeling as though you are talking to a wall. In this chapter the word *audience* may mean speaking to thousands at a conference center, a small group, your peers at work, or just one person. How do you break through to them? How do you make sure they get it? How do you highlight your point? It is time to give your message to them the *Lite-Brite® way.*

Just as all lightbulbs require an intact element to have light, communicating the *Lite-Brite® way* requires four elements: the lightbulb represents the idea, the black paper represents the filter, the colored pegs represent the delivery, and the viewer represents the audience. As you will see, all four of these elements must be present to effectively communicate your message.

The First Element: Let There Be Lite!

The first element is the bulb. The lightbulb represents the total intent of your message. It begins as a thought—just a glimmer in your eye. You decide to address an issue, ask for a raise, pitch your product, or deliver a passionate speech. You have all the thoughts running through your mind, but they are not yet ready to be spoken. Before you open your mouth, think about the intent of the message. As the bulb is lit, your thoughts may run in a million different directions, so you must organize them into one cohesive stream; it is here where you recognize people don't want to stare at a lightbulb without a shade, just like they don't want to hear everything you know about a subject in one sitting. Ask yourself, what is it that I really want to say, and what do I want the audience to do when I am done? Epictetus, the ancient Greek philosopher, said, "First, learn the meaning of what you say and then speak." That's great advice, even if it is about two thousand years old.

Your Message Won't Be Brite if There Is No Lite

Communication can be more complicated than you imagine when you assume everyone understands you when you speak. It is much the same when you stand over your golf shot. You imagine a perfect Tiger Woods swing as the ball flies high up in the air, lands on the green, takes one hop, and falls in the cup. You may imagine that on every shot, but just like the rest of us, you miss the green by fifteen yards when you actually hit the ball. In life, as in golf, there will be days that, in spite of your best efforts, your message will fail to hit the mark.

Are your ideas failing to capture attention? Are your thoughts rarely understood as you envisioned them? Are there times when you're just not sure you are connecting? The Nobel Prize–winning playwright George Bernard Shaw wrote that the "single biggest problem with communication is the illusion that it has taken place." Look at three types of situations where the light may have gone out. If you are not connecting with your audience, then it is time to check your bulb—it may be blown. When your communicated thoughts become cloudy or fail to inspire, then you may be presenting one of three dimly lit messages.

Ambiguous messages blow your bulb. Have you ever spoken to a group only to have them stare back at you like deer caught in the headlights? If so, you may be guilty of delivering a confusing or unclear message. This could be caused by too much or too little information. Perhaps you are thinking out loud before your light is totally lit.

One of the very best examples of an unambiguous speaker is Ronald Reagan. There was a reason he was called "the great communicator"—his ability to take complex issues and deliver them with incredible clarity was exceptional. You may remember these: "Shining city on a hill" or "Tear down this wall" or "I forgot to duck." Few leaders have demonstrated his gift for getting his ideas across to the listener.

To develop concise and clear communication skills, try this exercise the next time you get on an elevator alone. Describe who you are and what you do before you reach the fifth floor. If you can't, then work on shortening your answer while providing all the necessary information. Powerful leaders present crystal clear ideas. An ambiguous message will only guarantee that you will be ignored. Is your message ambiguous?

Untimely messages blow your bulb. People regularly plan a time to work, eat, and play, but many times they don't plan to talk. If your wife tells you the dishwasher is broken, the youngest child just threw up, and your mother is on the way to visit, now is not the time to tell her you are going to play golf.

Take a lesson from Abraham Lincoln when he was asked to deliver a speech at a Civil War cemetery dedication in Pennsylvania. The featured speaker, Edward Everett, president of Harvard University, delivered an eloquent speech for two long hours. When Lincoln took the podium, he delivered ten sentences in less than three minutes. Today that speech, the Gettysburg Address, is the most quoted presidential speech in history because its content was timely in purpose and in length.

Don't be guilty of presenting the right message at the wrong time or the right message that takes way too much time. If your message is important enough to verbalize, then wait for the moment when it will get the attention it warrants. Is your message untimely?

Irrelevant messages blow your bulb. Have you ever sat through a speech that reminded you of an old home movie? Or worse, someone else's home movie? You sit through thirty minutes of poorly shot footage of a baby falling down just to see him walk for three seconds. No offense to babies, but if he is not yours, then you don't care about the other twenty-nine minutes and fifty-seven seconds—cut to the chase. The same rules apply to communication. Don't ramble. Speak to the point and sit down. Your message should never be as irrelevant as someone else's old home movies.

> Your message should never be as irrelevant as someone else's old home movies.

If this occurs it is due to an unrelated or unnecessary message being delivered. At times, leaders think certain details are more important than the audience does. Before you open your mouth, put yourself in their seat to know what they need to hear. An irrelevant message wastes time, proves you are out of touch, and ultimately weakens your credibility. Include only your core message and leave them wanting more. Ask yourself, is my message irrelevant?

The Second Element:
A Filter Is Worth a Thousand Words

In January 2007, the *New York Times* ran a story reporting that the average American sees over two thousand ads every day.[2] Your mind has a smorgasbord of messages to choose from daily. That excessive amount of communication may seem a bit absurd until you think about how many billboards you pass on the way to work, the slew of commercials on television; then you are hit with ads at the gas pump, on shopping carts, and in a host of other places—all of them with one objective: grabbing your attention.

Just like you, your audience gets messages from so many places it is hard to process all of them. How then do you stand out from the crowd? How do you inspire as you communicate? How do you get people to focus on your message? You accomplish all of this by using a filter. For the Lite-Brite® toy, the black paper is the filter that blocks part of the light and lets the audience see just what they need to see. This occurs as you develop and organize your thoughts. At this point, they are not yet ready to be shared, but they are close. The difference between your message getting lost and your message getting through will depend on how well you filter the information you wish to communicate.

A Filter Makes Your Message Noticeable

The pegs poked into the Lite-Brite® box would blend into the grid if it were not for the black paper creating blank space covering the unused holes and preventing excessive light from getting through. The narrowing of the message makes the most important part pop, leaving out far more than is left in.

If you are not editing or filtering your personal communications, then all they may hear is "yada, yada, yada."

Beginning in 1994, milk mustaches appeared on billboards and in print ads using over two hundred celebrity faces. The minimalist message captured attention with the question: "Got Milk?" These ads were responsible for reversing a thirty-year decline in milk consumption and even made drinking milk popular. They made milk noticeable, and their message was received loud and clear.

A Filter Makes Your Message Compelling

Why should anyone listen to you? They won't unless your message is compelling. The key is to frame your message in a way that best benefits those who will hear it. What part of your initial idea will draw them in? Find that "hook" and they will listen.

The best way to find the hook is to organize your ideas. This is where you decide what will be black space and what will be light. What is relevant and what is unimportant? This organization comes through a pre-outline device like a web or mind map. A web or mind map is a diagram of words, thoughts, or concepts that are developed around a central theme. It is a way to record a free flow of information and ideas without the linear restraints of a traditional outline. Mind mapping will help you to "see" your thoughts and identify the part of your message that is most compelling. After a quick mind-mapping session, you can easily arrange a neat, organized outline that removes what is not needed.

The "Got Milk?" campaign did not say, "Do you want vitamin D, calcium-enriched, pure white, cold milk?" No, someone edited it down to the essence of their message. Some of the greatest communicators are remembered more by what they left out rather than by what they left in. Utilize a black paper filter to block out what is nonessential to your message and you will find what remains to be both noticeable and compelling.

The Third Element: Peg Your Point

The third element for a *Lite-Brite®* message is the pegs. Behind that black space is the light just waiting to emphasize the translucent colored pegs when they pierce the paper. If it weren't for the eight varieties of colored pegs on the Lite-Brite® toy, there would be nothing worth seeing. Those pegs represent your delivery. How colorful is it?

In our information-laden society, many leaders have forgotten the importance of an effective delivery in their daily communication. Lee Iacocca spoke about the importance of this when he said, "You can have brilliant ideas, but if you can't get them across, your ideas won't get you anywhere."[3]

Your message is worthless if you can't get it to your intended recipient. Having an idea is not enough. Having an audience is no guarantee. You need an effective delivery to be assured that your intent is received and, more importantly, understood.

When pegs deliver, the message becomes vibrant and excites the audience. And when the message is right, then people understand what you are saying to them. So if your message does not connect, you may need to change the bulb. In a world of bright lights, your message needs to be brilliant in order to outshine the other distractions around you. Delivering a message that gets the attention of the audience is your responsibility.

The delivery phase is where all the pieces come together to give your ideas life. It is the deliberate arrangement of the pegs in creative and repetitious patterns that form a powerful message. One by one, with each subsequent peg, the message becomes more and more clear. Likewise, you must choose a delivery design that is capable of appropriately concentrating your thoughts and thoroughly communicating your message.

One word of caution: whatever design you choose, make sure that your message is the focal point, rather than the design itself. Pick the right pegs, and blueprint your message to be simple, memorable, and focused.

1. Peg Your Delivery to Be Simple

Simplicity does not mean stupidity. Don't be afraid of it. In people's attempts to be elaborate or clever they often leave their audience confused rather than enlightened. Aristotle could deliver complex philosophical arguments, yet he understood the power of minimalism when he said, "It is simplicity that makes the uneducated more effective than the educated when addressing popular audiences." Advertisers understand this point. With billions of dollars spent each year on advertising, the most powerful design is often the most modest one. When you simplify, your message is much more likely to be received and understood by everyone.

> Simplicity does not mean stupidity.

2. Peg Your Delivery to Be Memorable

Craft your words so as to capture attention and facilitate recall. Attach your message to something tangible like an object or picture so the visual will reinforce the audible and inform the listener long after you stop speaking. Ask yourself, would I remember this if I weren't the one saying it?

The words you choose are but a part of making your message memorable. You should consider not only what you say but the way you say it. Phonetic cadence in a speech has long been a part of great communication. You see this used in speeches like John F. Kennedy's: "Ask not

> If your big speech is poorly written or apathetically delivered, then your audience might remember you, but it will be for all the wrong reasons.

what your country can do for you, ask what you can do for your country"; or Martin Luther King's: "I have a dream"; or Winston Churchill's: "Never give in, never, never, never. . . ." Each of these are memorable because of the pattern of the words that passionately deliver their message. If your big speech is poorly written or apathetically delivered, then your audience might remember you, but it will be for all the wrong reasons.

3. Peg Your Delivery to Be Focused

What is the objective of your message? You need a clear purpose when you communicate, whether you are introducing a new policy or telling your child to clean his room. To achieve this, you should be able to summarize your message in one short sentence. You cannot express your major points without clearly knowing where you want to take your audience. Failing to focus your message is like the difference between shooting a shotgun and a rifle. With one you pinpoint a specific target, but with the other you aim in a general direction and hope. Let your delivery be focus driven and you will peg your point every time.

○   ○   ○

A bright bulb, black paper, and a lot of pegs don't guarantee a pretty picture. It is the design that makes it work. If you cannot peg these three components in your delivery, then you're wasting your time and your breath. When you put these three pegs together, then you will be ready to understand the last major element: your audience.

The Outside Element: Influencing Your Audience

When you unpack the box and pour out the contents of a Lite-Brite® toy, you will find pegs, refill black paper, and a lightbulb; but one item you will not find is your audience—the receivers of your message. Do you remember completing your very first Lite-Brite® picture and yelling for a friend or a parent to take a look? It just wasn't complete until someone else admired your creation. Even as a child, you knew the best message in the world was useless without an audience to receive it. This is just as true today. To make sure your message reaches its intended audience, be sure you completely know them and adequately prepare them before you ever push the first peg.

Who's Listening to You?

Ultimately, communication is not about you but about your audience. So the more you understand them, the more likely you are to successfully get your message across. In his best-selling book *The Seven Habits of Highly Successful People*, Steven Covey writes that people often prescribe

> Communication is not about you but about your audience.

solutions before making the proper diagnosis when communicating. He says the habit that counteracts this is to "seek first to understand."[4] This habit is about discovering how people you are addressing see and hear the world before trying to get them to understand you.

There are lots of books written about how you should say things, but the vital ingredient needed to get your message across is knowing what your audience needs to hear in order to understand. Once you have identified that, you can address them at the level of their existing knowledge. When you really know your audience, you are able to tailor your message to their exact specifications. One last piece of advice: put yourself in their shoes and never forget to whom you are talking.

Are They Ready for You?

Before the first peg gets poked, you must know who will see it and what needs to be expressed for them to get the full impact of your point. Use these three checks to prepare your audience and, in doing so, prepare yourself:

1. Check the group: Who needs to hear this, and are they present?

2. Check the history: Do they have the context to receive this new information?

3. Check the setting: Is the environment free from distractions?

After establishing your audience's readiness, explore your core message, edit it down, and deliver it based solely upon your understanding of them. It takes a little extra time and work to go through the process, but the end result makes it worthwhile. Unfortunately, many leaders never realize that their audience needs to be prepared before the message can be received. Before your next staff meeting, public address, or dinner with your family, ask yourself these questions: Do I really understand them? Are they prepared for what I have to say? What needs to be done before I speak? Have I edited my message to fit the recipient?

Making Things with Light

At home or in business, success is dependant upon getting your message across. The ability to consistently deliver an intended message to the intended audience is the only way to establish and maintain productive and beneficial relationships. Painting barns in the twenty-first century looks considerably different than it did in Clark Byers's day. But the one thing that will never change is the importance of effectively communicating your message. Include the four elements of the Lite-Brite® toy, and your message will always be bright. So light the bulb, lay the paper, and peg your point! Only then will your audience see your message in lights.

Weebles®

ENDURANCE
Staying Down Is Not an Option

"Weebles® wobble but they don't fall down!" That's one of the most memorable commercials in toy history, but also one of the most misleading. The truth is, Weebles® toys *do* fall down. The trick is, they don't *stay* down. To understand how they work, you have to go all the way back to the nationally televised children's program *Romper Room*. The biggest-selling toy to come from that TV show was the Punching Clown, an inflatable "bop-bag" that had sand in the bottom. Punch after punch the clown kept going down and standing right back up.

When Hasbro acquired *Romper Room* in 1969, they looked to market this toy with a twist—they shrunk it and made it solid. On July 23, 1971, Weebles® toys were successfully introduced to kids and toy boxes everywhere. In the years to follow, they would have places to live, like tree houses and cottages; vehicles to drive, like cars and boats; and new occupations, like circus folk and firefighters. Many of the most beloved children's entertainers, like Mickey Mouse, characters from *Sesame Street* and the *Flintstones*, and even Santa Claus, found themselves transformed into the egg-shaped toys.

Their unique name came from their most distinguishing characteristic. They would "weeble and wobble," but they would not quit. Knock, throw, or kick them down, and you would find them in the same position they were in just moments before—upright. Weebles® toys teach durability, a mandatory characteristic for any successful leader. They teach you that staying down is not an option.

○   ○   ○

Nelson Mandela knows the truth of this principle. He went from being wrongly imprisoned from 1964 until 1990, to being elected president of a free South Africa. He summarized his life's testimony like this: "The greatest glory in living lies not in never falling, but in rising every time we fall." Your reaction to failure is important not only to you but also to those around you.

A leader is never more closely watched than in the moments following a failure. When leaders fail, you immediately wonder what their next move will be. How many times have you seen leaders respond inappropriately to failure or let it defeat them altogether? Just after the turn of the twentieth

> A leader is never more closely watched than in the moments following a failure.

century, one of history's greatest leaders, Ernest Shackleton, was a crew member on a failed expedition to reach the South Pole by crossing Antarctica. They used a ship named *Discovery* to try to get to the bottom of the earth. They turned back after realizing they were ill-equipped for such a trip. This failure taught Shackleton many lessons not only about planning but more importantly about how to deal with people under very demanding circumstances. He then raised a meager amount of money, packed more appropriate supplies, and set sail on the *Nimrod* to be the first man to reach the South Pole. A blizzard and limited rations contributed to another failure. He took note of what helped and hurt this attempt. Shackleton returned again to London, bought a very sturdy wood ship, and renamed it *Endurance*, after his family motto: *Fortitudine Vincimus*—"By endurance we conquer."

In 1914, with adequate supplies and rations, the *Endurance* sailed on what would be the most interesting sea tale you will ever read about. He would certainly wobble on this journey many times and ultimately fail at his goal, but leaders today have gleaned much from how Shackleton handled crises of catastrophic proportions. He kept getting back up after each wobble, and even though his ship was crushed in the ice and he was stranded in the frozen wilderness for two years, he still led his men out, while maintaining incredible morale. The book *The Endurance* chronicles Shackleton's extraordinary leadership skills and has inspired numerous other books on effective leadership. Shackleton exhibited the same quality that the Weebles® toys teach today—to keep getting back up through endurance.

Like Shackleton, you will fall down in life and leadership. The first step in getting back up is determining that staying down is not an option. Here are three endurance truths that will pull you back up each time you fall.

> The first step in getting back up is determining that staying down is not an option.

Truth #1: Endurance Recognizes That Falling Down Is Inevitable

When a child begins to walk and falls over, his father sometimes tells him to stop crying, to get back up, and to try again. It is not proper to expect that from a ten-month-old who has not developed a toughness in life, but as adults we must recognize the inevitable. Falling is a fact of life, but it doesn't have

> Falling is a fact of life, but it doesn't have to be the final fact.

to be the final fact. It all depends on your response to it. You can let failure grip you or you can get a grip on your failure. In *Failing Forward*, an excellent book on the subject, John Maxwell says this is the "one major difference between average people and achievers."[1]

Failure is inevitable and not necessarily bad. Many successes are predicated by failures or falling down. You simply must endure the lessons of failure on the path to success. Every leader gets knocked down, but for the leader who lasts, staying down is never an option. A good leader recognizes that when an employee makes a multi-thousand-dollar mistake, you don't let him go. You just paid for his education, and what he learned from that mistake will benefit him and your company.

Everyone falls. How hard you fall is greatly determined by your readiness for the fall. To ready yourself for a fall you must adapt these three prerequisites:

1. Anticipate the Fall

Good leaders know when things just aren't right. They can sense every wobble, and they know when a fall is coming. Your preparation will determine the severity of it. Have contingencies in place today. Anticipating problems determines how you handle people during failures and if they will follow you again. A good philosophy is to go into deals expecting them to work out but not counting on the payoff for survival.

Joe Frazier, the famous boxer, said, "The punch that knocks you out is the one you didn't see." If you see the punch coming, you can react. You can get out of the way or create a chance to at least "roll with it." It's when you aren't ready that failure hurts the most. The fall you didn't see coming can ruin you and your business.

2. Learn from a Fall

Good leaders have the ability to learn from both successes and failures. Walter Brunell calls failure "the tuition you pay for success." Don't waste the lessons that a failure can provide.

> In 1983, the Australian sailing team challenged the United States for the America's Cup. Despite America hanging on to the cup for 134 years, the Aussies directing their boat, Australia III, beat Dennis Conner's American entry in four straight races. It was a devastating and humiliating defeat. In 1988, Dennis Conner received about $5 million in return for endorsements. Why? After losing the competition back in 1983, Dennis Conner went back to the drawing board, built on his experiences, and won back the America's Cup in 1987. Conner and his sailing team learned from failure and rebounded to 'sail' to success.[2]

3. Don't Duplicate a Fall

What is the point of an expensive education if you don't learn from it? Occasionally when you fall it can be an expensive mistake. Getting the most benefit from your mistakes means using that experience to not repeat those same actions again. The British statesman Edmund Burke said, "Those who do not learn from history are destined to repeat it." Mistakes can ultimately make one wiser.

Truth #2: Endurance Requires a Center of Balance

It is not a coincidence that Weebles® toys look like eggs. This design is one of nature's most natural support structures. The shape allows for energy to be displaced throughout the toy instead of one part taking a direct hit. The shape acts in union with the low center of gravity. They have an inner center of balance and an outer shape that allows for recovery. Since every part of the construction is designed for support, every part is essential for it to automatically right itself.

Like Weebles® toys, every part of your being must assist you in getting back up from a fall. To achieve this you must maintain adequate support throughout your personal and professional life. A center of balance combines both internal and external factors.

Balancing Internal Factors

Rebounding from a fall starts on the inside. There are three personal or internal qualities required for a wide base of support.

1. Balance with determination. The climb back from a failure begins with one determined step. It takes determination to get back up again and again. "Determination is the wake-up call to the human will"—that's the way motivational speaker Tony Robbins sees it. Walter Payton was a testament to determination and getting back up after falls. In his NFL career he rushed for over nine miles. That meant that he had "someone knocking him down every 4.6 yards!"[3] Most people get back up once, some people get back up twice, but leaders get back up every time.

> Most people get back up once, some people get back up twice, but leaders get back up every time.

2. Balance with resilience. Guaranteed failure is choosing the path of least persistence. Resilience is defined as the ability to recover from setbacks. A more human definition would be the ability to bounce back from adversity. This is a quality that is birthed from determination and fully developed through repeatedly getting up after each fall. Weebles® toys, like us, do a good bit of wobbling; however, they are standing far more than they are lying down. Their resilience works to quickly get them back upright.

There is no limit to the number of setbacks you will encounter, but each setback will further define who you really are. Never be afraid of a lost step if the next two are forward. A man having consistent setbacks said to his friend, "It's like my car is stuck in reverse." The friend had observed the man was not learning from his mistakes and replied to him, "Friend, I don't think you're stuck in reverse. I think you are driving the wrong way." Don't be guilty of habitually making the same mistakes. General George Patton said, "I don't measure a man's success by how high he climbs but how high he bounces when he hits bottom." Resilience gives you the confidence and flexibility to bounce back higher each time.

3. Balance with purpose. The final inner quality you need for support is an understanding of your purpose. Possessing a clear sense of purpose will pull you up when nothing else can. Nineteenth-century British prime minister and legendary statesman Benjamin Disraeli called "constancy of purpose" the secret of any success. When you fall, remember your ultimate goal, your reason for being, and your personal destination.

Balancing External Factors

Just as the egg-shaped Weebles® toys has internal factors of weighting to help right itself, it also has an outer shape that enables it to rotate back into the upright position. An inner support structure alone, no matter how strong, is not enough. Even with the proper internal weight, you cannot succeed without the external factors working in cooperation with the internal. You need the assistance that comes from the outside. This outer or professional support can motivate you even when you inwardly see no hope. This is why the selection of people around you is so important. If vultures surround you, they will not be so eager to help you when you fall. If trusted colleagues are there, they will quickly respond to your need. Your exterior support will come from your people, your colleagues, your mentors, and your experiences.

Each of these will be a driving force in helping to right you in troubled times.

Support of colleagues. Every leader needs people in the organization who can give them honest feedback. People are often fearful to be honest with their leader because of the repercussions. Great leaders do not want "yes men" surrounding them. They want people who respectfully offer other perspectives and are thinkers for their boss. These people initiate potential solutions. You do not need people who require permission to perform their daily tasks or attempt something new. You want self-starters—people who fall down and do not need four e-mails and a policy describing how to get back up; they just do it. By recognizing that, leaders acknowledge success is not about themselves but is tied to something greater; it is tied to the people they serve. Allowing and supporting the failure of people around you also allows you to fail in their eyes without losing credibility. Each pushes the other to rebound quickly.

Shackleton, stranded in an Arctic wilderness, had lost his ship and had only the support of his crew to find their way out of this polar predicament. He and his men endured nearly twenty months of frozen misery, and morale ebbed and flowed. In one last-ditch effort, six of the men sailed for the mainland seeking help. The following excerpt from *The Endurance: Shackleton's Legendary Antarctic Expedition* by Caroline Alexander depicts the power of people who endured together, in spite of conditions, to overcome impossible odds. Having sailed eight hundred miles in a twenty-two-foot wooden lifeboat, they finally reached land.

"It was," wrote Shackleton, "a splendid moment." McNish's handiwork had stood up to all the elements had flung at it. Throughout their seventeen day ordeal, Worsley had never allowed his mind to relax and cease its calculations. Together, the six men had maintained a ship routine, a structure of command, a schedule of watches. They had been mindful of their seamanship under the most severe circumstances a sailor would ever face. They had not merely endured; they had exhibited the grace of expertise under ungodly pressure.[4]

Secure leaders will not be threatened by attracting capable followers to the organization. They understand that the value their employees add propels them forward in difficult circumstances.

Support of mentors. After a failure, who coaches you? Who cheers you on? Who listens to your thoughts? Who helps you understand? These are the duties of a mentor. You need a helper who has been through the fall before. You should have one or two mentors whom you go to on a regular basis. Mentors are sounding boards who offer guiding direction based upon their wisdom and experience. Your mentor should be someone you can expose your weaknesses to and who makes you stronger in those areas. Good mentors work themselves out of mentoring. Check chapter 3, "Play-Doh®," to see how mentoring gives and receives support.

Experience. Think back on your past experiences that include difficulties. The lessons you learned from them, whether work related or not, will help you with persevering today. Draw confidence from your past experiences. Looking back at this story from his days in the army, Ron finds motivation for today:

> There are two significant experiences in the army that motivate me today. Neither of these is a heroic action. When I was in basic training, squads were assigned daily cleaning tasks, and my squad was assigned the latrine (bathroom) used by the forty men in our platoon. When I left basic training and went to jump school, my squad was once again assigned latrine duty; so every morning I cleaned the bathroom. When I left jump school and went to rigger school, I was promoted to squad leader and yes, you guessed it, my squad had latrine duty. To this day, getting up from that experience with the right attitude has caused me to recognize that no task is

beneath my ability, and my wife often enjoys taking advantage of my military expertise when I clean our bathrooms.

The second experience was one of the longest nights I can remember. We were moving our entire infantry company of 160 troops, on foot and in full gear, across a swamp at Fort Benning. Just lifting a leg buried to the knee in the muck took a great deal of effort with every step. Each time I helped someone out of the mud, I only sank in deeper myself. I have found that the toughest times we face are not one bit enjoyable but will offer inspiration in days ahead, facing bathrooms and swamps, with different names.

John Maxwell tells a great story in *The Difference Maker* about a father helping his daughter understand how difficult experiences affect us. The father pulled out an egg, a carrot, and some coffee grounds. He explained that these three items teach us how we should handle difficult experiences. Boiling represents the difficult environments that affect each of the three items. The water makes the egg hard just as it does people when they are stressed. The water makes the carrot soft just as some cave to the pressures of life. The coffee grounds actually change the water, making the circumstances and atmosphere better.[5] What happens to you when life turns up the heat?

You will have the stimuli needed to withstand the initial shock of failure by combining the internal and external factors of Weebles® toys in an integrated support structure.

Truth #3: Endurance Results from Proper Weight Distribution

Weebles® toys are not top-heavy or flat on the bottom, but rather the weight is properly distributed. The position of the weight actually pulls the toy back upright. After a fall, the assistance you require will come from the places in which you have invested your leadership. The placement of your influence will determine the speed at which you recover. Allowing your team to risk and fail without harsh retribution will extend trust and confidence through the education of experience. Help them back

> After a fall, the assistance you require will come from the places in which you have invested your leadership.

up, knowing they will in turn help you. Share your experiences without rubbing in their failures. Show them how to get back up. Expect to weeble, be ready to wobble, and prepare to fall down. But determine, beforehand, that you will get back up again. Remember the caution of Edwin Louis Cole, founder of the Christian Men's Network: "You don't drown by falling in the water; you drown by staying there." Weebles® toys teach us that you are going to fall down, but they also teach us that staying down is not an option.

In his fifteen years in the NBA, Michael Jordan was a five-time MVP and six-time world champion. In November 1997,

Jordan appeared in a Nike TV commercial. He was walking into a packed arena as people chanted his name, "Michael! Michael! Michael!" Then he uttered this shocking statement: "I've missed nine thousand shots in my career. I've lost almost three hundred games. Twenty-six times I've been trusted to take the game-winning shot and I have missed. I've failed over and over and over again in my life." Then he added, "That's why I succeed."

Conclusion

You've probably seen it on a T-shirt or a bumper sticker: "He who dies with the most toys wins." It's cute but false. The real truth about toys is this: when you live out the lessons these toys teach, you can win today.

Now the floor is strewn with toys, and the toy box sits empty by the wall. Through these pages you have reacquainted yourself with some old favorites and perhaps been introduced to some new ones. What now? At times like these the earliest advice is often the best. In other words—what would your mother say? She would likely give you three commands: play with your toys, share your toys, and then put away your toys.

Use Them

Think about how many toys get unwrapped at Christmas only to be forgotten later in the bottom of some toy bin. Toys are only fun if they are being used. Likewise, the principles they teach are of value only when you implement them. You will always have your favorites, but to be a complete leader you need to utilize all of the lessons from these toys, not just the easy ones. You will never walk into a boardroom and announce, "Today we are going to play with the Mr. Potato Head® toy," but for you to be an effective leader, you must practice the principles he and the other toys in this book represent.

Share Them

When you were in kindergarten, one of the greatest compliments you could receive was that you "worked and played well with others." These kind words depended mostly upon whether or not you shared your toys. There was always that one selfish kid who gathered up his toys and went off to play by himself. Nobody liked him then, and nobody likes him now. You can avoid this fate by sharing the toys and their principles that you've read about here. When you make a habit of passing on the knowledge you have gained, that knowledge becomes much more relevant in your life and daily practice.

Put Them Away

Children's least favorite thing about toys is when playtime is over and cleanup begins. They reluctantly fill the toy box and keep their best ones on top so they will be ready for playtime tomorrow. They put away their toys, but they don't forget them. When you lay this book down and put away these toys, remember the lessons. Placing one of these toys on the corner of your desk or on a shelf in your work area helps you absorb its message and provides a constant reminder to focus on strategy, make new connections, continue to be mentored, or any of the other seven principles.

○   ○   ○

Toys simply and powerfully make the everyday lessons of leadership more memorable. Whether you are an executive, a manager, or a parent, you will find the toy box a great place to look for lessons to successfully influence and lead others. These ten toys are not all the toys in the toy box, but they filled the pages in this book right to the top. In the future, look for more playtime principles that will facilitate your leadership growth while continuing to have fun. There are lessons to be learned and principles to be practiced. So take out the toys, grab hold of the example, and watch them transform your leadership skills. Playtime is over—now get back to work!

www.toyboxleadership.com

Notes

Chapter One: LEGO® Bricks

1. Ken Blanchard, Interview with American Management Association entitled "Learn How to Bring Out the Best in Your Team Members by Bringing Out the Best in Your Leadership Ability," http://www.amanet.org/editorial/blanchard.htm.

2. Spencer Johnson, *Who Moved My Cheese?* (New York: Penguin Putnam, 1998), 51.

3. http://www.rolltide.com/ViewArticle.dbml?SPID=3011&SPSID=37423&DB_OEM_ID=8000&ATCLID=741887.

Chapter Two: Slinky® Dog

1. Laurie Beth Jones, *The Path: Creating Your Mission Statement for Work and for Life* (New York, Hyperion Press, 1996), 77.

2. Gordon L. Culp and Anne Smith, *Managing People (Including Yourself) for Project Success* (Hoboken, NJ: John Wiley & Son, 1997, 5.

3. Patrick M. Lencioni, *The Four Obsessions of an Extraordinary Executive: A Leadership Fable* (Hoboken, NJ, John Wiley & Sons, 2000), 168.

4. Neil J. Shipman, J. Allen Queen, and Henry A. Peel, *Transforming School Leadership with ISLLC and ELCC* (Larchmont, NY: Eye on Education, 2007), 119.

5. James M. Kouzes and Barry Z. Posner, *The Leadership Challenge* (San Francisco, CA: Jossey Bass, 2007), 14.

Chapter Three: Play-Doh®

1. Denzel Washington, *A Hand to Guide Me* (Des Moines, IA: Meredith Corporation, 2006), 8.

2. Louis L'Amour, *To the Far Blue Mountains* (New York: Random House, 1997), 84–85.

3. Mark Twain in *Speaker's Sourcebook II* (Boston, MA: Prentice Hall Press, 2002), 234.

4. http://www.leadershipnow.com/teachabilityquotes.html.

Chapter Four: Yo-Yo

1. David Állen, *Getting Things Done: The Art of Stress-Free Productivity,* quote from http://www.brainyquote.com/quotes/authors/d/david_allen.html.

2. Pat Williams, *How to Be Like Walt* (Deerfield Beach, FL: Health Communications, 2004), 232.

3. H. Jackson Brown, *Hero in Every Heart* (Nashville: Nelson Word Publishing, 1996).

4. Twyla Tharp, *The Creative Habit: Learn It and Use It for Life* (New York: Simon & Schuster, 2003), 7.

5. Williams, *How to Be Like Walt,* 243.

6. Everett M. Rogers in *Speakers Sourcebook II* (Boston, MA: Prentice Hall Press, 2002), 82.

7. Jeff Mauzy and Richard Harriman, *Creativity Inc.: Building an Inventive Organization* (Watertown, MA: Harvard Business School Press, 2003), 114.

8. Howard Schultz, *Pour Your Heart into It: How Starbucks Built a Company One Cup at a Time* (New York: Hyperion Books, 1999), 215.

9. Bob Kodzis, "Natural Born Creativity Killers," *Create,* Fall 2006.

Chapter Five: Mr. Potato Head®

1. Norman Wright, *Communication: Key to Your Marriage: A Practical Guide to Creating a Happy, Fulfilling Relationship* GLINT Ontario, CA 2000, 63.

2. Dale Carnegie, *The Art of Public Speaking* (Garden City NY: Knowledge Exchange Press, 2006), 169.

3. Andrew Beck, Communication Studies: The Essential Resource (New York, NY: Routledge, 2004).

4. James M. Kouzes and Barry Z. Posner, The Leadership Challenge (San Francisco, CA: Jossey-Bass, 2002), 16.

5. Pat Williams, *Paradox of Power: A Transforming View of Leadership* (Nashville: FaithWords, 2004), 49–50.

Chapter Six: Rubik's Cube®

1. Thomas Heath, "Companies Fear Spread of March Madness," *Washington Post*, March 16, 2006.

2. See http://www.rubiks.com/lvl3/index_lvl3.cfm?lan=eng&lvl1=inform&lvl2=contct&lvl3=faques&lvl4=10#69.

3. Jon M. Huntsman, *Winners Never Cheat: Everyday Values We Learned as Children (But May Have Forgotten)* (Upper Saddle River, NJ: Wharton School Publishing, 2005), 40.

4. David Callahan, *The Cheating Culture: Why More Americans Are Doing Wrong to Get Ahead* (Orlando, FL: Harcourt, Inc., 2004), 14.

5. http://coastalmanagement.noaa.gov/hazards.html.

6. Will Allen Dromgoole, "The Bridge Builder". PUBLIC DOMAIN

7. Enron's Code of Ethics, July 2000, 4.

8. Donald T. Philips, *Lincoln on Leadership* (New York: Warner Books, 1992), 52.

9. The Seven Social Sins, as quoted by Mahatma Gandhi in "Young India," 1925.

10. "Theodore Roosevelt and Integrity," *Today in the Word*, March 28, 1993. Taken from www.sermonillustrations.com.

Chapter Seven: Rocking Horse

1. dead horse list http://www.bpic.co.uk/articles/deadhorse.htm.

2. Todd Duncan, *Time Traps* (Nashville: Thomas Nelson, 2005), 100.

3. See http://www.conferenceboard.org/utilities/pressDetail.cfm?press_ID=2582.

4. Glenn Van Ekeren, *Speaker's Sourcebook* (Boston, MA: Prentice Hall Press, 2002), 212.

5. Mitch Thrower, *The Attention Deficit Workplace* (Guildford, CT: Lyons Press, 2005), 56.

6. Rosalene Glickman, *Optimal Thinking: How to Be Your Own Best Self* (Hoboken, NJ: Wiley and Sons, 2002), 9.

Chapter Eight: Little Green Army Men

1. Allan Cohen, James Watkinson, and Jenny Boone, "Herb Kelleher Talks about How Southwest Airlines Grew from Entrepreneurial Startup to Industry Leadership," Babson Insight Online. http://www.babsoninsight.com/contentmgr/showdetails.php/id/829

2. Tom Peters, *In Search of Excellence* (New York: Harper Collins, 1982), 122.

3. Bill George, *Authentic Leadership* (Hoboken, NJ: John Wiley & Son, 2003), 94.

4. Marcus Buckingham, *The One Thing* (New York: Simon & Schuster, 2005), 83.

5. Jim Collins, *Good to Great* (New York: Harper Collins, 2001), 13.

6. Collins, *Good to Great*, 57.

7. Larry Bossidy and Ram Charan, *The Discipline of Getting Things Done* (New York: Random House, 2002), 58.

8. Marcus Buckingham and Donald O. Clifton, *Now Discover Your Strengths* (New York: Simon & Schuster, 2001), 5.

9. John Trent and Rodney Cox, *Team Building Discovery Kit* (Nashville: Randall House), 2006.

10. John Maxwell, *The 17 Indisputable Laws of Teamwork: Embrace Them and Empower Your Team* (Nashville: Thomas Nelson), 33.

11. Andy Stanley, *The Next Generation Leader* (Sisters, OR: Multnomah Publishers, 2003), 96.

12. Jeffrey A. Krames, *Jack Welch and the 4 E's of Leadership: How to Put GE's Leadership Formula to Work in Your Organization* (New York: McGraw-Hill, 2005), 16.

13. Ken Blanchard, *The Heart of a Leader: Insights on the Art of Influence* (Colorado Springs: COOK Communications, 1998), 11.

Chapter Nine: Lite-Brite®

1. http://www.latimes.com/news/opinion/la-ed-boston03feb03,0,5379741. story?coll=la-opinion-leftrail.

2. http://www.nytimes.com/2007/01/15/business/media/ 15everywhere.html?ex=1326517200&en=a405e6d0cb65c00a&ei=5088&par tner=rssnyt&emc=rss.

3. Lee Iacocca and William Novak, *Iacocca: An Autobiography* (New York: Bantam, 1986), 16.

4. Steven Covey, *The Seven Habits of Highly Successful People* (New York: Simon and Schuster 1989).

Chapter Ten: Weebles®

1. John Maxwell, *Failing Forward* (Nashville: Thomas Nelson, 2000), 2.

2. Glen Van Ekeren, *Speaker's Sourcebook*, (Boston, Prentice Hall Press, 2002), 156.

3. Tony Robbins, *Illustrations for Preaching and Teaching*, 176.

4. Caroline Alexander, *The Endurance: Shackleton's Legendary Antarctic Expedition* (New York, Random House, 1998), 152.

5. John Maxwell, *The Difference Maker* (Nashville: Thomas Nelson, 2006), 105–06.

Acknowledgments

From Ron

I am the sum of all of these influences:

Pam—my best friend and partner in life.

You support my endeavors and the late-night hours of writing, and at times allow me to be a kid.

Michael and Lauren—thank you for playing with your dad and for making good decisions.

I trust each of you will continue to be leaders in your own way.

Randall House team members—you are the best team of passionate and creative people, who produce excellence every day.

Randall House board of directors—you are tremendous leaders and full of wisdom.

Michael—my coauthor and friend. Our strengths, vision, and creativity have always complemented each other.

My parents, friends, and other colleagues—for teaching me more than you thought you did.

Tim and David—my friends and mentors for many years. Words are inadequate.

From Michael

Thanks to Marianne, who reminded me of the importance of dreams.

Thanks to Dad, who reminded me of the importance of integrity.

Thanks to Mom, who reminded me of the importance of writing.

Thanks to Ron, who reminded me of the importance of teamwork.

Thanks to Tim, who reminded me of the importance of friendship.

Thanks to my three sons (Malone, Mack, and Manning), who reminded me of the importance of toys.

I would not be the leader I am without each of you in my life.

From Both of Us

We want to thank the team at Thomas Nelson who worked so hard on this book and especially our editors, Kristen Parrish and Heather Skelton, for cleaning up our toy box. We would also like to give credit to the many leaders and friends who continue to shape our lives.

About the Authors

Ron Hunter Jr.

Ron Hunter Jr. serves as Executive Director, President & CEO of Randall House Publications in Nashville, Tennessee, where his distinct approach to leadership touches new arenas through his creativity and vision. Previously, he served for eleven years in ministry in Florida and Tennessee and was co-owner of a full service advertising agency. Ron's military experience includes the Army's Jump, Rigger, Air Assault, and Infantry officer training schools. Today he travels nationally as a speaker doing leadership training and consulting. He has been married to his college sweetheart Pamela since 1987, and they are proud of Michael and Lauren their son and daughter.

Michael E. Waddell

Michael has experience as a minister, educator, speaker, and consultant. Traveling the nation, he addresses critical issues of life and business. Michael has a master's degree in communications, and his love for the subject is reflected in his writing and speaking. He currently serves as the chairman of the board of directors of Randall House Publications where his committee placement allows him to impact thousands of young people every year in matters of leadership development. Michael and his wife, Marianne, have been married since 1990. They are the proud parents of three boys: Malone, Mack, and Manning. You can contact him at michaelewaddell.com.